S0-ATS-547

Maria Isabel Pita

beauty
&
submission

BEAUTY & SUBMISSION
Copyright ©2004 by Magic Carpet Books, Inc.
All Rights Reserved

No part of this book may be reproduced,
stored in a retrieval system, or transmitted in any form,
by any means, including mechanical, electronic,
photocopying, recording or otherwise, without
prior written permission from the publisher and author.

First Magic Carpet Books, Inc. edition November 2004

Published in 2004

Manufactured in the United States of America
Published by Magic Carpet Books, Inc.

Magic Carpet Books, Inc.
PO Box 473
New Milford, CT 06776

Library of Congress Cataloging in Publication Date

Beauty & Submission By Maria Isabel Pita
$14.95

ISBN# 0-9755331-1-8

Book Design: P. Ruggieri

BEAUTY & SUBMISSION

Maria Isabel Pita

CONTENTS

PREFACE:
The Truth vs. Radical Stereotypes

For me – once the proverbial Catholic school girl – a good hard spanking possesses all the power and mystique of an unholy communion with the weaker aspects of myself it is my profound desire to exorcise. To be bent over the hard pew of my Master's knees as he prepares to spank me is to experience the breathtaking illusion of a divine hand being raised over me, and me alone. I think of a painful spanking as the hand of God because it descends from above like divine favor and divine punishment all rolled up into one inescapably powerful, and hauntingly heart-warming, statement – my body and my feelings (the flesh of my soul) are the mysterious nature of life itself being shaped and tamed so it becomes as beautiful as possible. Let me try and explain…

As a Catholic school girl, I knew beyond a shadow of a doubt that God loved me, and because He loved me so much, He had laid out certain rules I must follow for my own good; so I would not be led astray by evil influences and impulses that would ultimately leave me feeling empty by cutting me off from His love and the infinitely carefree beauty of my own eternal nature. Whispering into the dark screen masking the face of the priest behind it, I would confess to such small sins as yelling at my grandmother and losing my temper and smoking a cigarette without my parents' permission. The quiet male voice would then tell me to try and make an effort to be more patient with my grandmother and to never disobey my parents. The rather insultingly indifferent voice would assure me my sins had been forgiven and (disappointingly) my punishment always took the form of saying a few *Hail Mary's* and *Our Father's* before I left the church. I was sure a string of words recited from memory was not going to make me a better person; unconsciously, I craved a stricter discipline, which I was not getting at home either, for my father never once took me over his knee and spanked me. In fact, I was very clever at getting out of punishments. The few times I transgressed parental rules, I was always tearful and remorseful afterwards, as a consequence of which I was only grounded for one night as opposed to a week. My maternal grandparents lived with us until I was seventeen; I was thoroughly loved and utterly spoiled.

I traveled a long (and more often than not frustrating and boring) road from the time I wore a plaid skirt and a white shirt to the glorious day when a masterful man finally took me in hand and gave me my first spanking. Growing up, I had always been in 'control' of my loved ones, and so, not surprisingly, I ended up in a relationship with a man I could manipulate the way I had played with my Ken doll. It was during the interminable time we were together that I read *The Story of O* and suffered a revelation that terrified and thrilled me like a luminous arrow piercing the darkness of normality, after which nothing ever felt the same to me again. Ironically enough, I tried to play at bondage and domination with my living Ken, casting him in the roll of master as I explored my submissiveness. The game worked on a superficial sexual level only, and it was inevitable that the 'Frankenstein' I had animated with my fervent fantasies would one day strike out at its creator. His mainstream brain could not handle my increasingly perverse input, and one night, he struck me out of anger. We had been arguing in the bathroom, and as I picked myself up out of the tub it was as if my life up until that moment was sloughed off me like so much dirt and I was mysteriously new again. That blow was my punishment for letting doubts and fears rule my life and force me to live a lie. The years I had wasted indulging my weaknesses while my soul pined away in dreams were my penance, and now at last I could move on…

…To that glorious day when I felt as though my life really began in the hands of the man who subjected me to my first spanking. I was not expecting it; I could never have imagined how it would feel, and yet I felt as though I had been craving it forever. The sensual serpent coiled beneath the Virgin Mary's feet perched on top of the world had come alive in my mind through the black leather whips of S&M fiction, and beneath the first hard blows of a man's open hand on my ass, it was as if a boundless temptation was sliding up my thighs and flicking a divine hot tongue into my pussy. After leaving 'Ken' I found a job as personal secretary to a successful realtor, who also happened to be a master with years of experience in the lifestyle. He immediately discerned my latent submissiveness, and one morning when I was a few minutes late for work, he grabbed me roughly by the arm, pulled me into the small kitchen at the back of the office, and commanded me to bend over the counter. I was completely astonished, yet for some reason I found myself obeying him, and not even protesting when he lifted my skirt. When he yanked my panties down to my knees, I gasped, shocked by how intensely turned on I was, but it proved nothing to how I felt an instant later. He was a tall, well-built man; the three violent smacks he gave my ass were more than enough to inflame my tender virgin cheeks, and bring hot tears of pain and gratitude into my eyes as I breathlessly promised never to be late for work again.

My married boss became my first master, and even though he

never fucked me, he aroused my body to the point where I was literally weak in the knees and my pussy was juicing helplessly merely by spanking me. I was an incredibly sloppy slave, willful and challenging, completely unaccustomed to obeying commands without question (unless they pleased me) so I was spanked a great deal, and often severely. When he first took me over his knees, I hated him with all my heart and soul as he brought his rigid hand down over my defenseless buttocks over and over, until I had vocally repented to his satisfaction; however, I sucked his cock afterwards with more fervor than I had ever gone down on a man before, my pussy smoldering with longing. My ass was on fire, but what really hurt was the knowledge that I had richly deserved that spanking because my personality was still a selfish, frightened mess it was going to take a long time (and just the right man) to straighten out. Yet somehow I felt better than I ever had in my life after that first real spanking because the Powers That Be had finally taken me in hand by bringing this man into my life like a priest blessing me with the discipline my soul had always hungered for by way of my flesh.

Fast forward nineteen months to the day I was walking my dog, Merlin, and I met my soul mate in the grass – a botanist studying a rare form of palm tree that just happened to be growing in my neighborhood. After my married boss, I had been spanked a few times by a handful of different men, but only as a playful enhancement to sex, not as serious discipline. My true Master and I have been together for over two years now, and I have learned many wondrous lessons in that time I know for a fact have improved my character immeasurably. The tense discontent that stems from indulging the doubts and fears of my weaker self has lifted like a dark cloud off my psyche, and the hot lightning flash of my Master's open palm when he spanks me for my transgressions has everything to do with it. Now when the

Catholic school girl who will forever live inside me confesses her transgressions, the quiet voice of my Master assigns her penance before he carries it out relentlessly himself, not permitting me to wriggle free with desperate tears or to talk myself out of it with pretty remorse. My love for my Master is everything, and in his roles of 'priest' and 'daddy' he is really my best friend helping to give me just what I need to grow and develop as a human being.

As a Catholic school girl, I was essentially forced to compartmentalize my feminine being into the trinity of nun, whore and mother. Only my Master's love enables me to bridge the metaphysical gap between my religious and sexual natures as I seek to become the best and most beautiful slave possible, which essentially involves giving birth to a whole new self inside me. The first time my true Master spanked me, he had just given me my new slave name, Missa, and even though it hurt, his hand smacking my ass was also like a doctor's knowledgeable palm on a baby's bottom as its takes its first breath of a whole new atmosphere and way of being. Now every time my Master takes me over his knees, I feel as I did when I pulled out the hard yet cushioned rail in church to kneel and pray for the strength to always strive to be a better person so I could deserve to achieve all my heart desired. I don't believe in God as a man, but I do not doubt that Love is a divine force, so when my Master spanks me to punish me for not being the most beautiful slave possible, it feels very much like a divine hand silently telling me how intensely loved I am, as well as how painfully far I still have to go to be fully worthy of the boundless love that is the core of my existence. I know my Master must enjoy the feel of my soft ass cheeks quivering and warming beneath his blows. I know it excites him to have me bent helplessly over his knees and that he relishes having complete power over my body, yet I sense that the greatest pleasure he takes in spanking me is the knowledge that I am *letting* him punish me – that I *want* him to punish me – because I love him so much so I am always striving to be a better, purer vessel for love flowing between us. Somehow, every blow of his hand on the very bottom of my being makes me love my Master more than ever.

And yet spanking is only one of the ways in which my Master disciplines me while also giving me pleasure. I feel fortunate that I finally decided to read *The Story of O*. Suddenly, a secret door opened and I glimpsed a realm where all my deepest darkest most forbidden desires could all come true, yet for years I stood poised on the threshold, hesitating to take that first step to make my fantasies flesh. What I saw was a whole other world with radical laws I was mortally afraid of. My "normal" relationship with my boyfriend was frustrating but safe like Newton's law of gravity – I was afraid of falling and losing myself in that seductive black leather universe glinting with metal shackles like stars burning at the very heart of my sexuality. Too many extreme and distasteful things went on there and made me worry my submissive nature was like a cancer I had to fight so it wouldn't spread out of control and prevent me from living a normal, healthy life. It took years, and several more relationships, before I realized how wrong I was. I met the right man, who took me by the hand and finally led me through that conceptual door into the intensely exciting dimension of BDSM.

BDSM is shorthand for two distinct lifestyles that can but do not always necessarily come together. B&D stands for Bondage & Domination. S&M stands for Sadism and Masochism. One of the reasons I was afraid to explore my sexual submissiveness was precisely the BDSM acronym; I was worried one inevitably led to the other, which is not actually the case. Every BDSM relationship is as unique as the persons involved in it. What dominant and submissive individuals do together is determined by both of them. The idea that becoming a Sex Slave means being forced to live out the full and often extremely painful and offensive gamut of Sadomasochistic activities is completely untrue; it is a terrifying stereotype given birth by all the negative perspectives on sexuality so prevalent in our society. The force of organized religions that teach us to look down at our sexuality as a base animal instinct would like women to believe that if they are weak and wonton enough to venture into the devil-ish darkness of BDSM they will be damned into relinquishing complete control of their bodies and their right to say "no" to anything anyone wants to do to them – a traditional Medieval painting of hell but in no way an accurate portrayal of the sane consensual BDSM lifestyle I myself have been living for years.

Before I entered the lifestyle with the man I now call "my Master" as casually as other women say "my husband" I did not understand how controlled and consensual BDSM truly is. I really did not believe a Sex Slave could lead a normal, healthy human life. I thought my dreams of true love and my desire for a demanding Master were like matter and anti-matter canceling each other out. I have since learned otherwise, and written a detailed account of my "ascent into submission" as an intelligent woman with an independent spirit who is now also willingly and happily a masterful man's love slave. *The Story of M – A Memoir* is my version of *The Story of O* which very often turns women off as much as it turns them on because of how far it goes in destroying O's self-esteem. Paradoxically, a Sex Slave is in many cases a woman who knows and dares to acknowledge exact-ly what she wants. Absolute submission to love requires strength of character that is a far cry from the stereotype of Sex Slaves as mind-less *doormats* with no self-respect. The truth is every Slave is an indi-vidual, and even if some do indeed qualify as *doormats* the majority of the Slaves I've personally met do not. And this judgmental view of Sex Slaves as women unable to overcome abusive childhoods is as erroneous as the belief that all Masters are relentlessly cruel and heartless. Some Masters definitely are extremely sadistic as well as promiscuous, regularly dominating more than one woman, but it is also a fact that many Masters have only one beloved Slave. I am in such a relationship myself – I have no other Master except Stinger, and I am his one-and-only slave – and even though sometimes we're not monogamous in the traditional sense our bond is still completely exclusive. Some men give women engagements rings, Stinger forged a silver collar and lock for me to which only he has the key.

I must do whatever my Master commands me to, and yet there are countless things I would never consider doing no matter what. This may seem a paradox, but it's actually not, because the most important part of any relationship is trust; no woman should become the Slave of a man she does not trust absolutely. That is not to say it does not often take a long time for a Slave's mind and emotions to catch up with her heart and soul so she is able to obey her Master's commands without question or hesitation. I fell in love with my Master the moment I met him, but it took me months to trust him never to command me to do anything I didn't really want to. At first I was constantly afraid he would push me beyond my limits, but finally I realized that would never happen. The first thing my Master did when he collared me was ask me to choose my Safe Word – the word a Slave says when she feels she is being pushed too far either physically or emotionally, at which point whatever is happening comes to a complete and immediate stop. A Slave's Safe Word more than anything else proves false all the negative stereotypes of the BDSM lifestyle. A Slave's Safe Word proves that the mysterious heart of her Master's pleasure is to generously, and always very carefully, give her exactly what she needs. In *The Story of M* I wrote:

> I struggled with the term *Slave* until I realized it has no more negative connotations than the word *spirit*, which is only a label placed on a force transcending the mind. Some say the spirit is not real and that a slave has no life of her own and both may be true, or not, but that is beside the point. For me to be a Slave is to exist in a perpetual state of *love*, also another label for an invisible driving force. By this definition, a slave is not the lowliest creature on earth but rather an elevated being, for it all boils down to how much I love my Master that I am willing to do anything he says. The relationship between a submissive female and a dominant male is so ancient it is practically metaphysical in origin and nature. In the twenty-first century, when faith and marriage have degenerated into empty symbols, the terms *Master* and *slave* possess all the pure power of cosmic hieroglyphs branded into the human psyche with the same fire burning in the heart of the sun, sustaining it's beautiful 'slave' the earth.

In *The Story of M – A Memoir*, and now in *Beauty and Submission*, I am using my own experience to bridge the gap between the reality of the BDSM lifestyle and radical negative stereotypes. I hope I succeed in making it clear a woman should never feel guilty or afraid to explore her deepest, darkest desires, because the truth is you *can* live a "normal" life and enjoy a tender, loving relationship as a Sex Slave in the world of BDSM, where the only limits on your self-expression are what you and your Master desire to share together.

CHAPTER ONE:

Ancient Magic Makes the Best Present

A hauntingly large spider's web dipped in ink then curved around my flesh like the waves in quantum physics… a black web endlessly punctuated with tiny stars stimulating my fingertips where they glimmer on the four corners of diamond-shaped windows filled with the moon-white light of my naked skin… I've always had a metaphysical bent, and I languidly indulge it now as I bend my leg then straighten it again to caress the black fishnet stockings my Master gave me to wear with another of his many (forgivably) selfish gifts – a pair of shoes with tapering six-inch heels the unnaturally cold hot-red of blood mixed with frozen Vodka, for only in my dreams had I ever known a man so intoxicating until I met him.

Afraid of tearing the infinitely delicate fabric of fantasy, I always file my nails before carefully slipping my legs into the silken webs my Master loves to see and possess me in. Black fishnet stockings evoke so many things to me, but in his eyes I imagine they are simply the sensual net showing off his catch; his prize. My Master's desires are a dark Triptych of three scared parts revealing the goddess he loves to worship – a silver collar, black stockings, and excruciatingly high heels.

Safely away from sharp edges and rough surfaces, I fall back against my jade-colored satin comforter remembering other pairs of stockings sacrificed on the altar of lust in just one night, sometimes in only a few violently pleasurable moments; orgasms like a divine hand brushing aside expensive fabric-webs that took days to fashion… I recall sheer red stockings, lacy white dreams and shimmering violet creations, but my favorites remain the black silk stockings rising now against my Master's chest as his hands travel lovingly up and down my legs.

If I were to try and count the many times my Master has fucked me, it would be like gazing up at the night sky the way it really looks and not the way it appears living in the city, where just a few anemic pinpoints of light are visible here and there like the last remnants of neurological synapses in a dying brain. No, in just a little over two years, how many times my Master has made love to me already feels like the night sky the way it really is, impenetrably black and bursting with stars – an infinite number of beautifully violent explosions; cosmic ejaculations creating worlds. Of course my Master has come inside me only a finite number of times, but our desire for each other feels infinite. What does this poetic cosmic analogy have to do with the mindset of a sex slave? Everything, I say.

Once upon a time, when I was a relatively normal (extremely unhappy) woman who like many people just happened to read *The Story of O*, I was under the vague impression that sex slaves lived chained in dungeon-like cells at the mercy of anyone who desired them. At best they lived trapped in Victorian-style boudoirs in a sort of fourth dimension devoid of the gravity of personality and realistic needs and limits; the hot, sensually flowing dimension of an eternal orgasm. Of course, the exception proving the rule, there's no truth to that myth. Sex slaves live in the real world, in the sense that we obey the rules of gravity by enduring a daily routine, hungering for more than just hard cocks thrusting into all our orifices. Yet it's true that reading and thinking only serve to enhance the profound pleasure I take in my absolute submission to love. I've heard of slaves who are kept in cages like animals, of slaves who are always chained or naked, slaves who can only eat from a bowl while kneeling at their Master's feet. In my opinion these extreme scenarios fall into the realm of BDSM therapy, the lifestyle used as a form of shock therapy to heal old wounds of abuse, and there is great excitement to be found in growing inside. Nevertheless, extremes are not sustainable, and they are not what this book is about. *Beauty and Submission* chronicles my real day-to-day existence as a sex slave who essentially lives a healthy, so-called 'normal' life. And my Master and I truly do live such a life; we don't just present an outward illusion of doing so in the interest of social respectability which more often than not conceals profoundly frustrated and dysfunctional intimate relationships.

Right now I'm reading a book entitled *True Magick – A Beginner's Guide* #1, along with a *Discover Magazine* article about Antonio Demasio's theories of thought, and I'm finding them amazingly related. The practice of true Magic involves a trinity common to many sacred traditions. There is the Higher Self, the True Will or Soul; the Middle Self or the thinking mind; and the Younger Self or the emotional, physical being. According to Demasio, the body forms somatic markers – past emotional experiences that serve as guides for making decisions. Impaired emotions can have a devastating impact on an individual's ability to make rational decisions because they can't remember the feelings involved. '…The risk of emotional neutrality becomes greater and greater as the speed of cognition increases. There will be more and more people who will have to rely on a cognitive system entirely, without using their emotional memory, in order to decide what's good and what's evil… They can be told about good and evil, but good and evil might not stick. #2

Going back to magic and applying Demasio's theories... The information age (the morning, noon and nightly news) is digging a chasm between our mental and emotional selves and hence our true (higher) self seems only a religious myth of the innocent past. And what does this have to do with a sex slave, you may be wondering? Pain and intense pleasure – the undeniable physical, cognitive experience of experience itself; letting things sink in, developing personally vital somatic markers. The numbing power of the media has grown right along with me and inevitably deadened me emotionally in subtle but vital ways. Television-abuse reduces life to a spacewalk with a limited supply of oxygen inside your window to a world that makes no real impression on you whatsoever. In a sense, a good flogging can be said to be a ritual of magic in that it has the power to help me achieve the sacred marriage of my threefold nature; merging my physical flesh with my conscious desires. In another symbolic sense, my Master can be likened to the Middle Self, and as his slave I am the Younger Self; the love between us the very nature of the incarnate soul. There's an old ritual incantation, 'By the power of three times three, so I will it, so shall it be.' The question is, what is it that you wish to will, and what is it to truly be?

'Beauty' and 'submission' are two words, but they're really one and the same thing. For something to be beautiful it has to obey universal laws of harmony – obeying in the sense of embodying – so that as a slave obeys her Master she embodies the mysterious beauty of life and the world. Beauty is submission to the feeling we've all experienced deep inside us at least once in our lives even if only when we were very young – the unfathomable but undeniable sense that the universe is a magical place and our perceptions and desires are somehow the reason for it all. I've seen Dom's who to me looked like little boys showing off their sinister toy boxes. In many ways, the BDSM lifestyle appeals to those who still simply want to be allowed to play as adults and don't believe play should just be a child's privilege. I always wanted desperately to grow up so I could do everything I wanted to, but then when I reached maturity the world promptly sought to slap down this cherished illusion and wake me up to so-called reality. We're deceiving children by feeding them feasts of fun before sending them off to the executioner's block once they grow up. I read somewhere once that 'sex is the way adults play' and I think this is obvious, but what does it mean to play? As a child it involves being more than what you are; it means pretending to be something you want to grow into; it means adventures you want to have when you enter the real world as a grown up. When adults play during sex, we're donning metaphysical roles which can, in a sense, be called the real world of energies and forces supposedly beyond our control yet consciously embodied in us, and this is the real adventure.

Can there be anything more horrible than a bachelor party, a tradition that implies the unfortunate groom is prepared to sacrifice most of life's pleasures for love? Why must love seek to limit desire? If you're blessed enough to meet a person you want to spend the rest of your life with, it shouldn't end your life in so many ways; it should give you the power to experience the world as you never could before. Stag parties seem to say you can never really play again; that from now on you have to be good, responsible and dead. A white wedding dress is often a killing frost to human sexuality, but it doesn't have to be that way. The black tuxedo a man wears down the isle is the latently powerful darkness of space, and the white dress of his bride is the light, life and energy he commands, the cosmic otherness 'As above, so below' and the world is their oyster. There's no earthly reason why a man and a woman who love each other should have to sacrifice the excitement of sensual interaction with others. That's like winning the lottery and locking the ticket up in a safe with a hopelessly complex combination made up of countless cultural and historical forces which need to be cracked and broken through so we can fully enjoy our lives and relationships.

On greeting cards, sunsets are invariably peaceful and beautiful, yet in reality the sun is an extremely violent place that regularly suffers even more turbulent episodes. Sun spots generate giant eruptions of hot plasma and spew forth high energy particles. To me this technical description sounds delightfully pornographic. As children of the earth who would not exist without the sun, I think it is much more normal to have an intense, and often violent, sex life than it is to be romantically sedate, as a sedate (virtuous) universe does not really exist. And yet in a Master-slave relationship as in any other there also exist relatively quiet, peaceful zones surrounding and protecting the passionate core, just as outside its core the sun has a relatively quite radiative zone. 'Beneath the surface, this zone gives way to a much more turbulent convective zone that is constantly churning like a pot of boiling water.' Our desires and fantasies are perpetually churning just below the surface of our rational selves. 'This region is made up of hydrogen plasma, a gas of atoms whose electrons have been stripped away by the ferocious temperature, leaving just protons behind. The sun's magnetic field stretches the plasma into ropes that break through the surface and become loops or prominences. Nearly all the activity scientists see on the sun's surface... is governed by mysterious twists and turns in the field.' [3] My imagination scarcely needs make an effort to find these lines erotically stimulating, for I've often been stripped by lust's ferocious temperature, and had my naked limbs bound by ropes as I twist in turn in delicious protest while my Master enjoys his microcosmic version of a coronal mass ejection...

By the way, it is my Master who subscribes me to *Discover* every year. As an intelligent, curious, imaginative and creative (and not so humble) slave, I strive to bring together my threefold nature and look at things as I am doing now. For me, writing reveals the world to be full of fascinating parallels; things that don't seem related in the least are suddenly clear reflections of each other large and small through the pure magic of metaphor. Metaphor is another word for truth; truths revealed by the combined (magical) perception of our mind, heart and soul. Metaphors are their own dimension of significance existing alongside the three dimensions in which everything seems separate and objectively meaningless.

***

To briefly recap, my Master and I met in Miami. Less than a week later, he collared me as his slave and my training officially began. It is not an exaggeration when I say we fell in love at first sight. *The Story of M – A Memoir* is the detailed account of my ascent into submission, covering the events and emotions of the first gloriously tumultuous year I spent with my Master, Stinger. This narrative takes off where that one ended, shortly after we left Miami and came to live in northern Virginia, where my Master currently works as a scientist. I wrote, 'submission is a miracle of love that slowly becomes an enchanted state of mind' and it's true – I feel very different now, much more centered and at peace deep inside than I did when I finished *The Story of M*. I have been with my Master a little over two years now, and even though in *Beauty and Submission* I will describe our second year together in the same graphic detail, this book won't necessarily obey a strict chronological order; events will unfold as I feel and recall them, for so much of this second year has been about my efforts to achieve the Sacred Marriage inside me. If the first year was focused mainly on my technical training as a slave, and on shocking sexual encounters I never would have dreamed of having much less enjoying, the second year was mainly about absorbing everything I had learned and actually transforming into the beautiful slave I had envisioned becoming. My training continues in even more penetratingly subtle if outwardly less obvious ways.

Training to be a sex slave to a beloved Master has much in common with training to be a magician and can be equally dangerous, because if you don't succeed in at least initiating the Sacred Marriage inside you, you'll never make it on the path and you could seriously hurt yourself playing with such potent sexual and emotional forces. I received an e-mail today from another slave I find quite telling:

> *'Thanks Missa. I really did like your book. Mostly because it was the only one that I found so far that was about a slave's perspective when it came to training. I found myself so much saying, "Oh my goodness that's so like me" and mostly that came when I read your feelings on swinging as mine are quite the same and it is something that I have a struggle with after a year.'*

It's nice to know I'm not the only slave out there who's had to struggle with this issue. When my Master and I moved to up to the east coast, suddenly there were no on-premise clubs around to tempt us every weekend, and I must confess, I was profoundly relieved to be able to take a break from swinging, which my Master assured me we would have done whether we had been forced to or not. And the truth is that the longer we stayed away from the Lifestyle, the more I dreaded ever having to go back to it. It seemed the conceptual sword with which I had heretofore successfully battled the green dragon of jealousy had lost its mysterious edge, and

I was almost paralyzed with fear thinking about returning to the vitally exhausting sensual fray, so to speak. I would have to say that my Younger Self suffered from a fever brought on by suddenly finding myself back in the place where I had spent the first seventeen years of my life; we were living only a couple of miles away from the house in which I grew up. Suddenly, I was constantly, subconsciously reminded of my loving moral Catholic upbringing, the energy of which still permeated the atmosphere like a haunting radiation weakening me and my part in the vitally sensual relationship I had with Stinger. For a month or two I was strangely sick at heart as the part of me who had developed and experienced so much in the past year struggled with the little girl I had been. This little girl believed in true love, and against all odds she had finally found it, which is what made it so hard for me to accept that the forest of thorns was still there surrounding the castle of my dreams and that it always would be – all the painful challenges posed by Swinging. The thought of watching my Master fuck another woman; the thought of having to suffer another man's undesired cock inside me… at the beginning of our second year together all these thoughts cut me up inside more painfully than ever before.

It's difficult for me to write about this time now; it's like remembering an illness during which I was not completely myself. For a few months a part of me was weak and miserable as it battled the psychic remnants of my upbringing like a metaphysical virus. Fortunately my Master's energies at the time were very much occupied with his work as he adjusted to a fixed nine-to-five schedule, something he had never endured before. As I mentioned, there were no actual on-premise clubs in our new metropolitan area, and not having their threat looming over me every weekend was a welcome relief. I was nursing the mysterious emotional fever of reconciling my childhood with the present and the last thing I wanted to do was to try and scale the psychological mountain of Swinging. Otherwise, I was in heaven. At last I was once again living in a place where I could enjoy all the seasons, especially the invigorating cold weather I had missed so much in south Florida, where you're forced to survive almost year round in the unnatural climate of air-conditioning. Merlin (my beloved Shiatsu) Master and I moved into our new apartment on Tuesday, February 4th, and that week-end, on my birthday and our first anniversary together, the Lords (as I like to think of the Powers-That-Be) blessed me (and cursed everyone else apparently) with a record snow-storm. It's beyond me why people complain about snow when it enables them to stay home as we did, sitting by the fire sipping Chardonnay while the enticing smell of dinner roasting in the oven filled the apartment. With Merlin draped like a heavy white-and-gold fur across my lap, and my Master refilling my wine glass as he talked to me about his fascinating new position, and the snow falling in sheets outside tucking the whole world in like our own infinitely cozy bed, my life felt complete, and it was despite the hot erotic memories of Miami burning like the threat of hell in the back of my mind. But on that first weekend in our new home, enough snow fell to cool my torment by making it literally impossible for us to go anywhere or do anything except enjoy each other's company.

Shortly afterwards the cosmos gave me another gift in the form of my good friend and publisher, Richard Kasak. All my life (since I was five-years-old) I've been writing, and at that point in my career I had three erotic BDSM novels to my name while I slowly worked on what would become *The Story of M.* Thanks to Marilyn Jaye Lewis' posted announcement on the Sensual Romance website – which I joined in the belief that you need to give the universe as much raw material to work with as you strive to achieve your goals – I learned that the publisher of *Magic Carpet Books* was actively seeking quality erotic romance novels. To make a long story short, that's how I ended up with a contract to write an erotic romance set in Egypt entitled *Dreams of Anubis*. Most of the book I had already written as a novel of romantic suspense; all I needed to do was bring it up to my current standards, develop the plot, and add lots and lots of graphic sex. The same thing had happened in my life as in my work – I had never dared let myself go too far when writing sex scenes for fear of not fitting into an acceptable category, and yet it wasn't until a British publisher named Adrian Wilkins urged me to let go and write what I really felt like writing that I was at last able to get published. I did not set out to become an author of erotica, yet once I set off on that path, I mysteriously began to understand myself better and to realize my love life had suffered the same problem as my writing – I had forced myself to conform to wrong relationships out of fear of not finding a place and a mate in life – and yet it wasn't until I began admitting and defining to myself what I really desired and fantasized about that I put myself in just the right place and time to meet my Master.

I kept a journal the first year I was with my Master, and many passages naturally made it into *The Story of M*. The second year I was so busy writing erotic romances as well as *The Story of M* that, as a consequence, I neglected my journal; nevertheless, the way I feel about Stinger was everywhere expressed and described in my novels, so occasionally I will quote from them as though the passages actually come from my own private diary; in a sense that's what all my novels are even if the plot and characters are fictional. The following scene essentially describes how I feel every time my Master and I make love:

'Yes...' His strong arm around my shoulders inexorable as the law of gravity, I sat down on the edge of the bed again. He stood facing me, and I watched in a contented trance as he unbuckled his belt and unzipped his pants... I looked up at his face, and the firm shadows of his features softly carved by the lotus lamp seemed to fill all the empty spaces inside me... I reached up with both hands so he could cradle the sacred gift of his penis in my cupped palms as he pulled it out of his pants. He was only partially erect, which gave me a chance to savor the warm tenderness of his smooth, circumcised skin over the unyielding strength of his stiffening length. Remembering the drop of semen that had glistened from the rift in his head and reflected the rising stars in my dream, I grasped the base of his shaft boldly with one hand, relishing how rigid it already was in my grasp. The elastic of his underwear was shoving his balls directly up beneath his cock, and I lifted it up out of my way to lick the delicate fullness of his scrotum, noticing with appreciation that it was shaved. I heard both surprise and pleasure in his moan, and deeply gratified by the sound, I immediately slid his erection into my mouth, sucking on his head for a second to moisten my lips and make it easier to slip their tight ring down his full length.

'Oh Mary,' he whispered, and I sensed him deliberately resist the urge to take hold of my head with his hands. Instead he kept his arms relaxed at his sides as his penis grew even harder against my soft tongue. I remembered my dream and the way I had caressed my lover's head with the back of my throat, a skill no man had inspired me to develop in this life until now, for no other cock had ever tasted so good to me. The flavor of his semen was just right, as though it had been made especially for my tongue and taste buds. So many times in the past the flavor of a man's bodily juices had deterred me from wanting to please him this way for too long, but Richard's pre-cum was the mysterious foam on the intoxicating pleasure I took in swallowing his erection whole over and over again, letting him ride my face as my head bobbed up and down in the room's deep shadows. Every time the bulbous tip of his rigid shaft sank down towards my virgin neck, the satisfaction I experienced in burying all of him inside me was much greater than the slight discomfort...

I moaned in disappointment as he stepped back, sliding out of my devoted mouth. He shoved his pants and underwear down his legs, then just stood there looking at me. Part of me did not even think about sinking to my knees before him and pulling off the black leather sandals he was wearing before tugging his pants all the way off for him. They were heavy with his belt, and I didn't just toss them aside; I laid them carefully down beside his sandals, because even though they were not a ritually blessed loincloth, they still belonged to him and therefore deserved my respect as symbols of the flesh his soul had chosen to wear in this world. Then I stood before him and caressed the white shirt up his chest, savoring the complimentary contrasts of his tender flesh and the hard muscles beneath it. His skin was warm beneath the crisp coolness of his chest hair, which was just enough to give him all the exciting feel of a man without interfering with my kiss as I planted my mouth between the gentle swell of his pecs. I felt his heart pulse beneath my lips then he finished the job of pulling his shirt up over his head. Before he could toss it away, I took it from him and spread it neatly over his pants. He was completely naked now, and I seated myself on the edge of the bed again to take him in. As with his features, the proportions of his body struck a chord of perfection deep inside me. His broad shoulders and chest tapered down to an ideally slender waist and hips supported by strong, long legs that were just the right pedestal for the crowning glory of his fully erect cock.

'You're so beautiful,' I told him…

'You are even more beautiful,' he said. 'Lie back across the bed, my love.'

My love… the words seemed to give me a delicious shove across the firm mattress and make it easy for me to get comfortable against the pillows…

How much and how deeply I feel my Master loves me always gives me a delicious shove across the bed or the rug or the couch or a chair or my slave pillow, anywhere and anyway he wants to fuck me. And yet as I was writing *Dreams of Anubis*, the constraints of the genre, combined with the upbringing fever I have already described I was suffering from, began having a negative affect on my psyche. The heroine of my novel was allowed to sleep with more than one man as she searched for her true love, but with only one at a time, and anal sex was taboo along with only the mildest form of bondage. The girl I was writing about found true love (as I had) and experienced intense, profoundly fulfilling sex (as I had) but she wasn't forced to play with other women or to share her soul mate with them, and once she met the man she truly wanted, she never had to suffer another cock inside her. In other words, Swinging was not a thorn in her paw she was constantly worrying over and conceptually licking in order to somehow learn to live with it. Yet after the first couple of months in our new home (during which, as always, I communicated my feelings to my Master, who invariably listens attentively and knows just what to say) I began growing paradoxically restless even while still finding myself reluctant to face all those sinfully hot Miami memories. But I was beginning to feel more like myself again – more like Missa, the name given me by my Master to symbolize the birth of my new self. Missa was to so many aspects of MIP what a profoundly confident ancient Egyptian queen was to a fear-ridden milk-maid serving at a convent in the Dark Ages. And the fact that my psychic health was returning began to find its way into the book I was writing in small but obvious ways that reflected the conflict between Missa and MIP inside me:

'I sense Mary Fallon and Nefermun at each other's throats, and Mary is afraid of losing a part of herself in awakening another, but there's no need to be afraid, trust me.'

I clung to his voice, which was both infinitely soft and firm, listening to what he had to say for all I was worth, whoever I was.

'Nefermun is an ancient priestess. Mary Fallon's personality was shaped by the twentieth century, and so she believes her rational mind is to be worshipped above all her other feelings and perceptions. But pure reason is a limited, fear-ridden deity, my love, and I know your heart is pure and powerful enough to see past the pragmatic, money-worshipping culture into which you happened to be born this time around. Do you understand what I'm saying to you, Nefer-marymun?'

'Yes!' I whispered fervently. 'You make complete sense to me, Richard. Your mystical beliefs strike me as totally logical.'

'That's because they are, logic of a higher order. Do you like your new name, Nefer-marymun?'

'Yes… it feels right.'

'Mm…' He pressed his hard-on against me, cradling it in the small of my back. 'You feel right, just right.' He turned me to face him abruptly, his possessive grip tightening on my arms. 'Nefer-marymun,' he whispered.

'E-Ahmose…' I savored the ancient name on my modern tongue and liked how sweet and familiar it tasted. Our breaths wrestled together for a moment before his lips pinned mine down and slowly parted, teasing me with the promise of his tongue and another deep, spiraling kiss. Then I was distracted from our silent conversation by the feel of his hand lifting my dress up in front, and slipping between my legs. I moaned into his mouth as he cradled my soft pussy in his hard palm, feeling my sex lips bloom eagerly against the branching lines in his skin. I sincerely hoped that what lay in his future was touching me like this again and again forever. I cried out softly as he thrust his index finger into the moist heart of my vulva while at the same time gently crushing my clitoris beneath his thumb. The summit of my mound was caught in the vice of his grip, and the pleasure was almost painfully intense as his hard thumb rubbed up and down against my clit in rhythm with his finger penetrating me swiftly and rhythmically.

'Oh God, stop,' I begged.

'Why?' he whispered against my cheek. 'Doesn't it feel good?'

'Oh yes, too good…'

He laughed. 'How can anything feel too good, Nefer-marymun?'

'I don't know!' I wrapped my arms around his neck and clung to him. The sharp ecstasy cutting up through my pelvis made me feel as though he was lifting me off the floor in the devastatingly powerful cradle of his thumb and forefinger.

'I want you to come for me again, my love. Soon you'll learn to come without touching yourself,' he promised. 'The more times we come together and you let go of all your tensions, the more sensitive your clitoris will grow until it learns to respond to the subtle friction of my cock as much as to the slightest touch.'

'Oh God,' I groaned, loving what he was saying as much as what he was doing even though I still felt it was too much pleasure too fast for my body to handle. Then I let out a small scream when the door leading out into the hall crashed against the wall as someone kicked it open.

Simon's man cut a menacing figure in a long black robe, and there was something threateningly sinister about the white crescent of teeth he flashed Richard.

E'Ahmose, Priest of Anubis, did not react as I expected him to by pulling his hand out from between my legs and letting my dress fall around my ankles. Instead he behaved as though we had not even been interrupted.

'Richard,' I gasped, 'there's a man-'

'You're going to come for me, Mary,' he said calmly.

I glanced over at the intruder, whose initial defiant grin was dimming to a look of disbelief as he eyed my naked thighs and Richard's hand working between them. I had never been in such a position before, and something strange was happening inside me... I realized with a shock that it was seriously turning me on to be skillfully fondled by one man while another man watched. Our observer's penetrating stare somehow touched me inside in a crucial spot at the very heart of the pleasure induced by Richard's relentless caress, and I came, all my defenses collapsing around the strangely arousing fact of how sensually open I still was even though we were no longer alone...

'Mm, yes, that's it,' Richard purred in my ear as I climaxed in his hand, burying my face in his neck so as not to witness my own wanton behavior.

It was a loss when he pulled his hand out from between my legs and took a decisive step back that forced me to slip my arms from around him.

He held my eyes as he slipped his glistening index finger between his lips and sucked off my juices before turning to face the man still standing in the doorway as if paralyzed by what he had just witnessed. Crossing his arms over his chest, Richard regarded our dumbfounded audience with an expression that appeared passive, but the contained power I sensed in his absolute control thrilled me.

It's obvious from this passage that I craved the thrill of an audience during sex; that aspects of Swinging turned me on as much as they did my Master and I was being unfair to both of us by believing it was something I did strictly to please him. (A good way to destroy any relationship, whether it be between a Master and slave or a husband and wife, is to blame your partner for something you can't admit to yourself.) And yet it's true that, like Mary, I sometimes didn't quite believe in my body's ability to experience constant sexual pleasure. I didn't think I had it in me, and I was afraid this sex slave business would get to be too much for me and I wouldn't be able to respond with a true sense of arousal. I was not accustomed to being erotically charged 24/7 and I was afraid I would short-circuit emotionally if my Master pushed me too far. I was afraid, I was afraid, I was afraid… why was I so afraid? I don't even know now. All I know is that by the time I finished writing *Dreams of Anubis* I was Missa again and aching for exciting experiences to share with my Master, and I was grateful to him for having gently but relentlessly forced me to overcome my inner demons:

This had to be the inner door Richard had referred to, the 'bolt' was fear, and until I found the strength to draw it, the way to heaven and the luminous flame of my invulnerable spirit was closed to me. Lying naked across the lid of a sarcophagus in a pitch-black burial chamber, my soul understood and appreciated this ancient invocation in a much more intimate and vital way than just casually reading it on a plane. All I had to do was lighten my heart by letting faith burn away the fears clogging my metaphorical arteries, or something like that.

At some point, I found myself not only forgiving Richard for leaving me here alone in the dark but actually thanking him for forcing me to face myself as I never had before. And remembering the way he had looked at me after we made love on this very same sarcophagus lid banished the demons haunting me and filled me instead with a reassuring sense of his presence. Suddenly, the darkness was not a formless threat, it was the mysterious depth of his love embracing me.

'I love you, *E'Ahmose*,' I dared to whisper the truth out loud. 'I love you, Richard!'

Eventually, amazingly, I felt myself drifting peacefully off to sleep. He had promised he would lead the way into our shared dream, and I didn't want to keep him waiting too long…

I can feel the heat of the sand through my gilded sandals.

My power is a presence surrounding my body and I am fully accompanied by it now as I walk deeper into the temple. *Re* descending behind me caresses my bare shoulders with his penetrating heat, a little less ardently in the dry season. I am wearing only jeweled sandals and a pure white dress, for you can take only the magical flesh of your soul into the darkness ablaze with dreams. I know the rite in which I am to participate is performed every cycle on the night the divine crook of the crescent moon first appears in the evening sky, and I am looking forward to it, as I look forward to everything with *E'Ahmose*...

I sensed myself shift restively against the cold stone on which I was lying, refusing to let go of the priestess walking through the temple merely to indulge a few minor physical discomforts...

Nefermun has reached the hall growing vast stone papyrus stalks where *Re* stretches long golden arms between the columns to embrace the priests and priestesses of *Anubis* preparing to worship his dark spirit. Vividly painted hieroglyphs bloom metaphysical vines all the way up to the star-covered ceiling as in a final flood of light, the god completes his circuit of the heavens and plunges into the black earth. In the same instant every man in the hall spreads himself on his back across the stone floor covered with blood-red runners, while every woman lets her dress feint into a pool of moonlight next to the body of her lover. I am one of these women, and for a few moments I gaze around me at my sisters. They are all beautiful in their own way, different garments of flesh and blood woven by *Hathor*, goddess of love. *E'Ahmose* lies still as *Osiris* beneath me as I admire all the lovely pairs of breasts exposed to the invigoratingly cool temple air. From small and pert to full and heavy, every firm yet luscious bosom is oiled to a golden perfection shining in the light from braziers being lit around us. Naked servants whose black skins blend with the darkness make it seem as though the flames spring to life of their own volition, and they walk away so silently on their bare feet the illusion is complete. Priestesses never bear children, so all my sisters' bellies and hips are as taut as *Khnum* fashioned them on his potter's wheel, and to me it is obvious his hands lingered lovingly on the round cheeks of their buttocks, but especially on the ripe bud of flesh between their legs containing all the delights of earth. I love looking at other women's bodies that are as sensually graceful as mine knowing they are feeling very much the same thing as I. During the rite, our combined sensations will flood the space between the stone papyrus stalks in invisible yet irresistible currents of pleasure lapping with a swiftly deepening power between our thighs. But only part of my attention is concentrated on my fellow priestesses, for most of it is devoted to the splendid sight of my priest's shaft surging straight up from the soft mound of his groin, and then to the sensation like no other of planting it inside me as I lower myself over him, my sandaled feet resting on either side of his hips. In this position, holding my back perfectly straight, I can feel the lips of my sex gaping open, and the tender petals of flesh protecting the darkly moist mouth of my flesh gladly accept the crown of his stiff penis, longer and thicker and harder than any vegetative stamen. He does not move a muscle as I mount him, seemingly alive only his erection, which becomes everything to me as it fills my belly. Continuing to hold my back straight with my arms crossed over my chest, I can tell from the soft cries rising around me that I am not the only one overwhelmed by the experience of slowly stabbing myself. I must sink all the day down around him, taking his hard cock so deep into my body the fulfillment is excruciating as I crouch like a woman giving birth to the divine soul of ecstasy as we merge completely, and then hold utterly still for a brief eternity…

Gasps of mingled effort and pleasure echo mine as all the other priestesses willingly impale themselves while opening their arms wide to spread the invisible wings of love over the inert men below them. Reflecting *Isis* resurrecting *Osiris*, we hold our torturously arousing positions until the temple floor seems to come to life as all the priests suddenly move as one. There is no choreography now as every couple does as it pleases surrounded and observed by other beautiful bodies consecrated to the dark god *Anubis*. The strong shoulders and chests of the other priests are all embracing me when *E'Ahmose's* beloved arms come around me, yet he is mysteriously more than just one of the powerful physiques I see thrusting their erections deep into the holes of moaning priestesses. And as I watch them, the all-consuming sensation of my lover possessing me from behind jackal-style is intensified to the point where all the gasping, groaning energy in the hall feels devastatingly concentrated between my own thighs. My mouth opens in hungry sympathy observing a rampant penis penetrate a lovely upturned face held possessively in the man's hands. Then I see a couple only one column away who seem a reflection of *E'Ahmose* and me, and I find it intensely exciting watching the girl's breasts bobbing swiftly back and forth just like mine are doing as our lovers ram into us. My

Priest of *Anubis* is feeling vicious tonight, and I love every moment of his strong body beating against me. My sex is slick as perfumed oil and hot as the pulsing flames when he grabs me by my finely braided hair, and makes me face in a different direction so we can watch other couplings together. The blessed suffering of his cock once again spearing me is almost more than I can bear, especially combined with the vision of another rock-hard column of flesh disappearing into the soft depths between two slender legs. It is the sound of his balls slapping against her helplessly juicing sex as he pumps in and out between her widespread thighs, and the sight of her delicate breasts quivering beneath the onslaught of his selfish thrusts, that make the shadowy temple vanish in a blinding flash of joy for me as the seed of divinity bursts open in my womb and for a few timeless moments I glimpse what paradise will feel like…

CHAPTER TWO:

Starz In The Crucible

T rue to his word – that once I scaled this particular hurdle in my training it would come up much less often – my Master has only taken me to a Swing club four times in twelve months, although we have also played with other people in private, always a much more enjoyable and fulfilling experience. Websites such as Adult Friend Finder (AFF) and alt.com (for those rare Lifestylers into BDSM) are an essential resource in the Washington D.C. metropolitan area where there are no real on-premise clubs to speak of. My Master and I didn't quite realize what this meant at the time we joined STARZ, a swingers club in D.C., where 'open minded couples seeking an alternative lifestyle gather regularly to enjoy life's pleasures to the fullest... where the capital's finest come to shine.'

At the time we joined, STARZ was meeting every Saturday night at the 'Party Place' in Manassas. Our membership card came in the mail, and after months of abstinence, my Master and I prepared for a night that involved more than just going out to a nice restaurant. I was excited and terrified, desperately clinging to my Master's assurances that there was absolutely nothing for me to be afraid of. I couldn't quite believe him. He didn't appear to be at all worried about any of the nasty gremlins I clearly saw hiding behind the naked limbs of the dark forest he was leading me into, my high-heels making me even more vulnerable to all the creepy people who might reach for me. I knew he would protect me, but I also knew he would consider letting me be used, and the certainty of the former battling the fear of the latter made it impossible for me to relax. I had no idea what to expect from this completely new venue, and this compounded my anxiety to the point where my emotions felt like a cave full of sleeping bats the slightest misstep would awaken with devastating consequences to my submissive self-control. I was determined to keep a tight rein on my highly skittish feelings, but how handsome my Master looked in elegant black slacks and a white button-down shirt didn't help since there was the chance he would not be riding *me* all night; since there was the chance I would have to let another man slip into my pussy's slick saddle, and God only knew where I would end up inside if that happened and I didn't like it. Another disorienting factor was how different my Master looked when he released his beautiful long hair from its perennial ponytail; it gave a dangerously sensual edge to his personality that wasn't quite as pronounced when we were being cozy together at home, and even while his flowing mane excited me and made me feel like being wild with him, it also paradoxically made it harder to get a grip on the part of me afraid something might happen that would throw me off balance and maybe break something subtle yet vital between us.

I hate writing about this now. Trying to remember and describe how I felt that night is worse than running a fine-toothed comb through tangled hair frizzing into a highly unattractive anxiety, my Master's smooth reassurances able to smooth only the surface of my inner turmoil. At least on the outside I looked fabulous. I was wearing a red bodice I had bought in Brazil that gave me the torso of a fairytale princess, the tight waist and deep cleavage enhanced by flowing transparent sleeves attached to the stiff, beautifully worked bodice. A loose black mini-skirt, and delicate red-and-black sandals with four-inch heels completed the ensemble, my long black hair waving around my ivory-powdered face (it had been a long time since we lay beneath the Florida sun on the nude beach) shocking red lips and smoky eyes. Once we were underway in the jeep, my Master kept glancing at me and telling me how beautiful I looked even though my body was now hidden inside an ankle-length red coat. I was pleased, but at the same time the difference between my outward beauty and the mysteriously ugly doubts, fears and resentments secretly churning inside me like a witch's cauldron (the opposite of true magic which seeks inner balance) made me seriously unhappy.

It was a long drive up to the 'Party Place' even if an easy one on Route 66. We didn't get lost until we hit endless dark back roads in the middle of nowhere. The directions we were following were very strange in that our goal was listed as CP Travel. I shivered as I held the flashlight up over the paper feeling like a treasure hunter who would rather go home and stay safely poor.

'How can there possibly be a club out here?' I demanded, my snappish tone making me feel even less attractive, which further aggravated how tense I was. We ended up driving right by the place without even realizing it since it would never have occurred to us to look for a swing club called the 'Party Place' in an industrial business area. But that's where it was, and we discovered the meaning of the CP (I had vaguely wondered if it stood for Corporeal Punishment, even though that made no sense since I knew perfectly well STARZ was a vanilla swing club) when we pulled up in front of CP Travel. Unbelievably, these northern swingers met every Saturday night at a small travel agency. I think Stinger was as shocked as I was, although he concealed it with his usual masterful self-control. After he paid our fifty-dollar admission, he hung our coats up on a rack near the door, then hand-in-hand we proceeded to explore the only swing club in our area. Despite my fairytale bodice, I imagine I looked very Egyptian with a smile painted on my lips beneath eyes widening in shocked disbelief as I took in the narrow corridor that clearly belonged to an office during the week. There were the two requisite bathrooms, but all the other doors were closed and locked, except for one at the very end. My Master opened it curiously, and my hand clenched around his in horror. The STARZ playroom was a small empty office across which had been spread a thin white bed sheet. That was it; that was all.

I said, 'Oh, my God' or something to that effect, plus a whole lot more, I'm sure, albeit in an appalled whisper as we continued the painfully limited tour. The other half of the club consisted of a narrow area with chairs against one wall and a make-shift bar set up against the other – i.e. a fold-out table covered with a black cloth. There would have been a lot more room if it wasn't for the bulky exercise equipment shoved into one corner. This narrow socializing area opened onto a very small wooden dance floor flanked by a steep staircase leading up to the only decent area of the club – a small 'living room' boasting a real but completely empty bar with four stools; two black leather couches; and a big white bearskin rug. Large black-and-white photographs of New York City hung on the walls, and a television was silently playing the requisite XXX film.

I never would have thought to find myself feeling nostalgic for *Miami Velvet* or *Plato's Repeat*, but I was suddenly missing south Florida. We had arrived relatively early, and the handful of couples present struck me as being almost conservatively dressed. Obviously, living in D.C. was going to prove somewhat of a culture shock for a Master and slave hailing from America's hedonistic capital.

'I need a drink,' I said.

'Good idea,' my Master agreed, and still hand-in-hand we made our way back downstairs to the 'bar' where an overweight middle-aged blonde woman poured us both vodkas on ice from the bottle we had brought with us. Yet I knew all the vodka in the world wasn't gong to make a small travel agency theoretically transformed into a Swing club for one night look or feel good to me. But my Master was determined to have fun with me there no matter what, so we went and sat upstairs on one of the comfortable black leather couches, where we sipped our drinks and tried to make the best of the situation.

'I'm just happy to be out with you, Missa,' my Master told me, his arm draped around my shoulders. 'We don't have to come back here, but we *are* going to have some fun tonight.'

'Yes, Master.'

'I love showing you off, and you know how much I love fucking you in public… Mm, I really miss fucking you in public, Missa.'

It wasn't long before I was kneeling in front of him contentedly watching him unzip his slacks then pull out his cock so I could suck it. There were several couples standing and sitting around who I imagine watched me going down on my Master, but all I could see when I opened my eyes was the crumpled black space of his pants and his rigid shaft; it doesn't take long for my Master to get hard, especially when people's eyes caress his erection along with my hands, lips, tongue and throat. I could have glanced around me every now and then if I'd been so inclined, but I wasn't; I hadn't yet seen a couple I found appealing. On my knees with my face buried in my Master's lap is one of my favorite places on earth, particularly in a club when I feel myself surrounded by other bodies that don't appeal to me.

'Thank you, Missa, that's enough for now,' my Master said,

somehow slipping his stiff, glistening penis back inside his pants. 'Now it's your turn. Take off your skirt.'

I knew better than to protest. I slipped my skirt down my legs, and even though I scarcely admitted it to myself at the time, I relished the touch of strangers' eyes on my naked assets. It was a sensation I hadn't experienced in a long time, and apparently my body had missed it; already I felt pleasantly languid as I took my Master's place on the couch and watched him kneel before me.

I sank comfortably low on the leather cushion and kept my heels on the carpet as my Master's talented tongue went to work on my cunt in public. There were more people milling around now, and forcing myself to look boldly up at my surroundings, I suffered an unexpected thrill. The members of STARZ were all mostly so conventionally dressed I could almost forget I was in a Swing club, which made having my pussy casually eaten in a crowd strangely exciting. It always feels good when my master's mouth and fingers are working between my thighs, and my gaze teasingly meeting those of men standing around me mysteriously brushed my clitoris in tandem with my Master's tongue in a way that almost made me feel I could come. Almost, but not quite, and I was glad when my Master seated himself beside me again on the couch.

So our first night at STAZ progressed. I think we danced for a while, and a few hours later inevitably found me on my hand and knees on the bearskin rug while my Master fucked me from behind. The white fur was pleasantly soft against my cheek as his ramming thrusts forced me down into the sleen position.

'Young people, how they love to fuck,' someone sitting at the bar said as they watched us. 'You've gotta love 'em.'

And I loved having my Master all to myself, even though earlier in the evening I had seen a couple who interested me. He was a tall, muscular black man, and she was a relatively attractive blonde. Nothing had come of the eye contact I made with him on several occasions or rather nothing good had come of it. Swing clubs are full of intense emotional undercurrents my Master seems blithely unaware of or simply unconcerned by, but I am always sensitive to the feelings flowing around me, and especially to feelings surging directly against me, as I felt this blonde's doing every time she caught me eyeing her man. How tense and uncomfortable she looked perched beside him on the edge of a coffee table (for lack of a better place to sit) made me feel contrastingly centered and in control of myself. The amorphous terrors I had suffered earlier as I showered and dressed at home, and then during the long drive, had vanished in the face of the reality, which was intensely disappointing but hardly frightening. Once I was actually at the club it felt like awakening from a nightmare about a big test, which is never so bad even if it is difficult simply because in your fears you're powerless, whereas in reality you have all the power you dare to possess and make exciting use of. This woman obviously didn't want to be there, and even though I was a touch disappointed, I wasn't surprised when they left the club soon after arriving.

All night I vaguely cherished the hope my Master would not make me suffer the indignity of taking me into a 'play room' that was only an empty office with a bed sheet spread across the floor, but of course I knew he would, and of course he did. We slipped our shoes off out in the hall as the hand-written sign indicated we should, and then my Master opened the door onto a writhing mass of bodies. I gasped inwardly. Every inch of the uncomfortably hard floor seemed to be taken. I thought longingly of *Velvet's* dark-red mattresses and of *Plato's* cushy leopard-skin beds as Stinger led me into what felt distressingly like a jar of worms all crawling mindlessly (not to mention soullessly) over each other. We found a spot (just barely) against a wall, and wearing only my bodice, I dutifully positioned myself on my hands and knees so my Master could fuck me from behind, a position that enabled us both to look around. I was not inclined to do so, however, and kept my head down, yet I was so appalled by where we were that I was very nearly impossibly aroused by it. My Master obviously was; his cock was so hard it felt glorious sliding in and out of my always welcoming pussy. Then, inevitably, a hand reached for me, and I sighed as I relished my Master's response to his slave being caressed in the increased urgency of his thrusts. I knew what he wanted; I reached out with one hand and reciprocated. The woman was not beautiful, but her breasts were round and heavy, and there was something about her dark eyes as she looked up at me from the floor… she was gazing at me almost worshipfully as she reached gently into my bodice to free my breasts while I fondled hers as best I could with one hand, bracing myself against my Master's driving penetrations with the other.

'You're so beautiful,' she whispered in wonder, and I moaned as we kissed, our dark wavy hair mingling. She was wearing a series of ancient-style bead necklaces, and as I reached up to stroke the smoothly shaved head of her handsome, tattooed partner, I was aware of falling into a mild state of trance… the pulse of my Master's thrusts was suddenly happening somewhere outside normal space and time as the woman I caressed took on the appearance of a Bodhisattva lying peacefully on her side even as her partner stabbed her mercilessly… full hips curving into a delicate waist crowned by perfectly round breasts almost too heavy for her slender frame… I had seen this body countless times before in museums and photographs of Indian temples, and it was as though I was being blessed by the Bodhisattva of pure sensual pleasure on that hard floor in an empty office – a secular space suddenly touched by an aura of erotic enchantment. With her meltingly dark eyes fixed lovingly on my face, I was able to admit to the hunger I had suppressed for months and was still so afraid of – the hunger my Master and I both sometimes feel for sensual contact with other people together. When my Master is inside me, it's as if our feeling becomes one, so even as my hands fondled the woman's breasts I felt him experiencing the sensation with me, and it is this intense connection between us I find more arousing than anything while we're playing. When the Bodhisattva's partner suddenly pulled out of her and got up to greet a couple who had just walked into the now 'standing room' only sexual arena, I was glad she stayed with us, almost seeming indifferent to his absence as she continued worshipfully caressing me. I don't remember if I asked her for permission or not, but soon I had the pleasure of watching two of my Master's fingers sliding in and out of what I was glad appeared to be a tight little pussy as his cock thrust in and out of mine, doubling his pleasure. I glanced over my shoulder at him and I'll never forget how beautiful he looked with his shirt unbuttoned, his features at once softened and sharpened by the same almost mystical rapture I was experiencing.

The enchantment began wearing off when the woman's partner returned and tried to get me to take off my bodice. Then Stinger shoved his hand away as he tried to finger my clit.

'Careful,' my Master told him, 'you can touch her, but carefully; she's very sensitive to fingers.'

Suddenly, I couldn't believe how afraid and worried I had been earlier that evening. How could I ever doubt that my Master loved me and would protect me?

Impossibly enough, we enjoyed a few transcendent moments in

that empty office turned Swing club, but they didn't last long. A pair of bare black feet planted incongruously in front of my face, the uncomfortably hard floor, and the completely unappealing atmosphere, soon made my Master decide it was time for us to go, thank the Lords.

***

The day following our first night at a Swing club after months of abstinence, my Master and I both felt as though we'd had our brains massaged; we felt perfectly relaxed and content and, if possible, more in love than ever. His constant assurance that Swinging really is all about us was beginning to sink in. We had played only with each other last night (except for the brief period of fondling fun with the Bodhisattva) and he was obviously just as happy as I was with the results. We had both needed a relaxing night and Swinging was like a trip to the ocean, sexual waves surging into the bottle of a small office better than nothing. We had dipped into a sensual sea of humanity in which my Master's work-related stresses and my subjective fears were temporarily washed away. Nevertheless, my Master agreed with me that the 'Party Place' would only be tolerable on an occasional blue moon. I was happy to hear it, for I seriously doubted I would be able to experience another enjoyable trance-like state on the hard floor of an empty office covered with a thin white bed sheet. I could still scarcely believe I had been one of the bodies fucking in that room, albeit not a completely naked one as I sought to preserve some sem-blance of dignity and personality by keeping my bodice on. I was appalled at the lack of effort made by the owners of STARZ to provide a more erotically stimulating atmosphere for their patrons; it struck me as disrespectful, to say the least. They have since cleared out the exer-cise equipment and added blue air mattresses to the playroom (which, however, they don't bother trying to make more sensually appealing in both texture and appearance by covering them with sheets) but the 'Party Place' will always be a travel agency at heart, and the best thing that happened to STARZ was when they made a deal with the management of *The Crucible*, a BDSM nightclub in D.C., to rent their space out once or twice a month on Saturday nights. Needless to say, Master and I were excited about the possible ramifications of this unlikely combination – swingers forced to mingle in a venue filled with kinky toys. At the very least we could enjoy playing with the BDSM equipment and shocking quite a few vanilla sensibilities in the process.

***

Everything about going to a Swing club is invariably a shock for me; the place and the people never live up to my imaginative expectations. *The Crucible* was almost as hard to find as an alchemist's obscure equation, and if I had cherished the hope that a kinky environment would help transmute the base metal of Swinging into something more, I was, naturally, disappointed. I should have realized after our first STARZ experience that these tough northern swingers – forced to thrive in a politically correct sensual desert – could be amazingly indifferent to their environment; striving to create an erotic oasis wherever possible. At least *The Crucible* was actually a nightclub and not an office.

That night my Master looked absolutely devastating. He was wearing black leather pants into which he had tucked an off-white long-sleeved shirt evocative of past centuries in its slightly rough cotton texture and the threads tying the sleeves, and the space over his chest, loosely closed. He also had on a heavy black belt, his black combat boots, black leather metal-studded half-gloves, and his long, silky hair was down. Just looking at him made me want to sink to my knees and worship him, but secure in the knowledge that I would be doing so soon enough, I was able to control the impulse and walk calmly beside him, my hand resting comfortably and safely in his as always. My feet weren't quite as comfortable in my favorite six-inch black vinyl high heels with the closed toes and school-girl-shoe straps, but I had long since learned to walk in them, albeit slowly and very carefully when ascending stairs. I liked how tall they made me, almost putting my face on a level with my Master's as we stepped into the unknown realm of a new venue. I was wearing my Catholic school girl's outfit – an indecently short plaid skirt beneath a long-sleeved white silk shirt half unbuttoned down the front to reveal a Gothic cross hanging between my naked breasts. The man at the front desk took one look at us when we walked in and immediately declared, 'You're not STARZ members.' He believed us to be part of the home *Crucible* crowd, which of course we weren't, but it was expressive of the fact that my Master and I always seem to fly a unique course between the sensual worlds we explore, only briefly intersecting with them at certain points.

The Crucible is located in an industrial lot adjacent to a very bad neighborhood in D.C.. It is nothing more than a large warehouse to which the trappings of a nightclub have been added, but after the 'Party Place' we weren't about to complain about the spacious first floor, large enough to hold a small dance floor on one side and to accommodate delightful BDSM equipment everywhere else. In the shadows at the back of the club loomed a couch and chairs and a flight of stairs leading up to a smaller second floor comfortably furnished with more couches and chairs, as well as bar stools placed before a railing looking down at the club. There was no one up there yet in what was clearly the play area for STARZ members, whereas for the *Crucible* crowd it appeared to be where they went to relax after making use of all the bondage equipment below. Some of the kinky apparatus scattered across the first floor included a table on chains, the purpose of which rather eluded me; a wooden throne-like chair with wrist and ankle straps attached; a plush leather 'vaulting' bench; straps hanging from an iron frame where a slave could be tied and whipped; and (my favorite) a beautiful black wooden cross. There also appeared to be straps and pulleys for suspension hanging from the ceiling, and lifting the edge of a dark purple curtain revealed a small, smoke-filled room with a pool table. On both sides of the curtain stretched fold-out tables neatly covered with sinister items all for sale at astronomical prices – floggers, blindfolds, shackles, nipple clamps, you name it, the *Crucible* staff was selling it. The members of STARZ avoided this dark display rather like tables in a doctor's office full of potentially painful tools. They were clearly proud of their normal healthy sexuality and looked askance at these rather sick extremes of pleasure combined with pain. My Master and I were not in need of any of the items on display as he had made most of them for us himself out of quality materials bought for next to nothing at flea markets, but we enjoyed perusing the mysteriously appetizing black leather and metal buffet. I, for one, felt we had too much time to kill before the party got going, after which we would thankfully be going. My Master has often commented on my extreme skittishness, and I do often feel like a thoroughbred he's leading gently but forcibly along by the dual reigns of love and desire, calmly holding me down whenever I threaten to rear and run.

Our tour of the club concluded, we walked over to the area in front of the small bar and sat at a table while waiting for the place to fill up. There were no empty tables, so my Master asked a woman who was sitting alone if we could share hers. She said 'Yes' and glanced around her as though anxiously looking for someone, avoiding making eye contact with us. At the time, the one major draw-back to the *Crucible* was the fact that no alcoholic beverages were allowed on-premise. The management has since corrected this problem by procuring the proper Permit, but that night they were still in Bureaucratic limbo, which meant that whenever I wanted a drink I was forced to make my torturously slow way outside to the jeep across a gravel parking lot to sip tepid Vodka. I was as happy with this arrangement as a patient forced to undergo a painful operation without anesthesia, and this in turn was something Master was not happy with.

'You shouldn't need alcohol,' he insisted, 'you should just be happy to be here with me, Missa.'

I looked at him incredulously. Surely he wasn't serious? I don't remember what I said exactly, but I know I made it clear he was asking too much if he expected me to be able to relax in a place like that without a few drinks. In my mind, his disappointment in me for feeling this way was totally unreasonable, which prompted me to resent him for making me feel inferior to his water drinking, utterly relaxed self, which led to a whole series of negative emotional reactions inside me that exploded as a fierce disgust and furious jealousy when he struck up a casual conversation with the woman at our table. She was the quintessential vanilla swinger – a middle-aged bleached-blonde with the leathery skin that comes from being penetrated by the sun's rays for too long and too often coupled with bad genes.

When does pride cease to be the solid foundation of your self-esteem and become the weakness of vanity and the agent of your fall? As a sex slave, I have pondered that fine line many a time, because I always seem to walk that tumultuous fault whenever my

Master takes me to a Swing club. My Master asked the woman a question about the drinking policy at the Crucible, and I immediately imagined he was interested in fucking her, which disgusted me on a purely physical level, and then made me blindingly angry at his willingness to 'slum it' when he already possessed a woman so much more beautiful and desirable in every sense. Describing the tempest of my feelings in those moments is like trying to analyze every painful bit of destructive shrapnel involved in an explosion. I went completely cold towards my Master and rudely ignored the woman, who was thankfully collected by her partner a few minutes later and fled the table. I didn't blame her. Then I really felt like a patient on an operating room table denied the blissful numbness of anesthesia as my Master angrily but patiently searched for the root of the pain that was causing me to lash out at him. I hated myself for my lack of self-control – which always led me to assume things then to react to these assumptions as though they were facts – and the heart of this profound illness of my psyche was the dangerous tumor of the fact that I was still constantly underestimating my Master in every sense.

I felt raw but at least momentarily cured of my mental agony by the time we finished talking about the incident. My Master accepted my need for a few drinks to help me deal with situations I found difficult, so to this end we headed out to the jeep for a few minutes. I perched on the front seat with the door open and took several desperately hearty swigs of Vodka from the still thankfully cold silver flask. My Master stood watching me with appreciation for my beautiful intensity warring with a somewhat frustrated concern on his remarkably handsome features.

'You know,' I said, given a sudden hot courage and clarity by the powerful spirit, 'I really wish… it would make coming to Swing clubs less frightening for me… if you would think of oral sex as a very special favor we bestow on other women… I mean, I really don't see how you can just go casually down on every woman you get the chance to go down on. Not only is it not safe, it's… it's disrespectful to me… I mean, I get the feeling you feel the same way about eating my pussy as you do about eating any other pussy, whereas I have absolutely no desire to go down on another man at all!'

'Missa, if you're going to have a tantrum, we can just leave right now…'

'I'm not having a tantrum!' I said desperately. 'I'm just trying to communicate how I feel to you. You said I was always to tell you what I was thinking and feeling, right?'

'Yes…'

'Well, I think I would be a lot less terrified of Swing clubs if I thought you were going to be more discriminating about licking pussy. I'm afraid that every time we go to a club I'm going to have to watch you going down on one or more girls, and I dread you're going to make me do it too, and I just can't stand the thought of so much casual oral sex. I need to know you're going to be more discriminating in the future, that's all.'

'Missa, for one thing, you're doing what you usually do and letting your fears make you assume you know what I'm thinking and planning on doing. The fact is I've never given you any reason to feel that way, have I? If I'd licked every pussy I had the chance to lick, I would have licked a lot more pussy, don't you think? No, listen to me… you're doing what you always do and not trusting me. You don't trust me to be in control of situations and to never make you do anything you really don't want to even though we've been together over a year and I've never given you a single reason to feel that way. Have I really ever done anything to hurt you, Missa?'

'No…' I shook my head miserably. I knew the problem wasn't

with my Master, it was with me and my fear that if I went so far as his slave I would have to go all the way and do things I knew for a fact I could never tolerate. I had come a long way in a year, but I still did not have complete faith in my Master to only take us as far as we both desired, not just wherever he wanted to go at my expense. If I had fully trusted in the mysterious marriage of our souls, I would have known that whatever he desired would never be more than I could give. And he knew me better than I knew myself; I knew perfectly well that, consciously, I was often afraid to admit just how far my desires could go.

'I agree with you,' he added more tenderly as he saw me absorbing his words and struggling to take them to heart, 'we should be discriminating about who we honor with our oral attentions, but I'm disappointed you can't seem to tell the difference between the way I go down on other women compared to the way I go down on you, Missa.'

'I'm sorry!' I whispered, quickly relinquishing the cold flask of Vodka for the warmth of his shoulders as he helped me out of the jeep.

'Just stop letting your fears run away with you, Missa, and trust me.' He held me against him. 'All you have to do is trust me,' he murmured.

'Yes, Master!' I sighed, knowing it was much easier said than done. It was still the beginning of our second year together, during which I have finally truly learned to completely trust my Master. In order to do so, I had to perform some serious magic inside myself – I had to unravel the painful emotional knots left by another man who had selfishly bound me to him for ten years because I had been weak and afraid enough to let him. It hasn't been easy freeing my self-esteem (and the love and trust that is the very air it breathes) from all the psychological convolutions of my upbringing and previous relationships, but my Master's love and understanding have affected me like divine hands massaging my soul and profoundly relaxing me into my true being.

***

The rest of our first night at *The Crucible* was intensely enjoyable. When there were a sufficient number of people around to watch, I finally had the pleasure of being tied to the cross by my Master. He had brought a duffel bag full of his home-made leather cuffs and floggers, and he used two of the former to secure my wrists. I was bent at the waist with my back straight and my ass offered up for punishment as he lifted what there was of my skirt up out of his way. I found it a strangely exhilarating experience to behave as a slave at a social event not consecrated to expressions of the BDSM lifestyle. I was aware of a couple standing near the cross watching as my Master disciplined me, but for the most part my long hair formed a dark, private curtain around my face as I hung with increasing languor from my bonds. My Master started out slowly, using a variety of floggers as he gradually increased the force and the pace of his blows. When he paused to whisper in my ear, 'Are you all right?' my fervent response assured him I was doing much better than fine; with every sharp, hot kiss of the lash my pussy was getting hotter and wetter. I began feeling as if there was no bottom to my submissive depths or to how much I adored my Master, who had never looked more beautiful than he did when he at last released me from my shackles, although I almost didn't want him to. I felt I could have held that pose for hours – my back arched and my perfectly straight legs braced on the pedestals of my obscene heels, my body essentially held up by the cuffs and by the delicious arousal suffusing my whole being. Afterwards, my Master didn't need to tell me to sink to my knees before him and suck the cock he pulled out of his black leather pants for me. The whole experience was like a choreographed dance in which I smoothly and inevitably ended up on my knees gratefully worshipping his erection; relishing the mysteriously wonderful taste of my Master's pleasure on my tongue like a communion.

When he took my hand and helped me to my feet, I willingly followed him up the steps into the now crowded play area, docile as a child. Suddenly being surrounded by naked fucking people felt utterly natural in my sensually primed state; the prolonged flogging had enveloped my senses and perceptions in a deep mist of contentment obscuring any clear thought except the only important one – how deeply I loved my Master – the other side of this priceless coin how much I longed for him to fuck me. When he bent me over a clear spot on one of the couches, the pleasure of his hard-on thrusting into me from behind was indescribable, and the harder he fucked me the deeper my pussy seemed to become in profound gratitude at being host to his uncompromisingly forceful and passionate penetrations. At other times when my Master fucks me so violently I have to make an effort to relax around him, but that night, after being ritually beaten on a cross, my sex felt divinely hot and endlessly accommodating.

I kept glancing at a skinhead with a black goatee on the other side of the couch who was wholly engrossed in his partner, grateful to have a handsome man in my line of sight as my Master banged me from behind. Then he had me sit on the cushion so he could go down on me, and for a few moments I enjoyed the attentions of another man whose girlfriend was bent at the waist as his dick stroked her cunt and his eyes caressed me. Yet being pleasured orally was nothing compared to the dark joy of being flogged and then violently fucked, and I tried to let my Master know he was wasting his time and energy. I was happy to soon find myself on my knees again facing him where he sat on an armchair beside the balcony. I took in one last glimpse of the club below – I was interested in the scene of a woman wearing a topless black leather corset and extreme high-heels like mine being gradually suspended in a crouched position that would make both her ass and pussy available from behind and her mouth accessible from the front – before I began sucking my Master's cock for all I was worth. I had never yet made him come just with my mouth, and I did not consciously set out to do so then, but gradually I became vaguely, deliciously aware that I was deep-throating him like never before. The flogging had loosened me up inside in more ways than I would have believed possible; I was swallowing his penis whole over and over again and still feeling hungry for more and able to take it. I could tell some-thing wonderful was happening when I felt my Master's slick erec-tion pulsing the way only my other orifices had enjoyed before. But now my sucking lips and swirling tongue and caressing throat were achieving what only my pussy and my ass had had the honor of doing. I was aware of a blindingly hot few instants, and then I real-ized I had succeeded in what I had begun to fear was impossible – I had brought my Master to a violent climax just with my mouth. My happiness and sense of triumph new no bounds as he stroked my hair and quietly praised me. I scarcely remember what he said I was feeling so transcendentally smug. I still cherish the memory of his cum flowing straight down my throat.

For me the night was now more than complete, but if my Master is wonderfully virile in private, in public he can be exhaustingly so. I was still destined to be fucked from behind some more right beside a man who stroked himself avidly as my Master rode my pussy mere inches from his jealous face. But at last it was time to go, and I had to admit I preferred one thing about northern Swing clubs as opposed to Miami venues – the fact that they close at two o'clock in the morning instead of five o'clock. Whenever my Master's cum has baptized more than one of my orifices the universe seems to vibrate at a different, much better frequency as all the cells composing my feminine being purr contentedly. It was in this state that I entered the bathroom to relieve myself before the long drive home. As I stepped out from behind one of the white-curtained stalls, the bodice-clad redhead I had watched suspended, and then pleasured by at least two women, walked into the bathroom.

'You look fabulous!' she exclaimed, or something to that effect, her green eyes appealingly dreamy.

'So do you,' I said, politely returning the compliment even though it wasn't quite true since she looked pretty, but not fabulous; however, she would more than do as a potentially promising catch I could drag out to my Master and lay at his feet.

She asked me for my name and seemed inclined to try and write all my information down on a scrap of paper she fumbled out of her purse.

'Go ahead,' I said, indicating she could pee first, 'I'll be outside' which is how I ended up exiting the bathroom in smiling triumph waiting for her to emerge so I could present her to my Master. I'll call her Daisy, and her Master, who stepped up a moment later to introduce himself, John. I did not like the looks of John at all; there was something I can only describe as skanky about him. Then I became confused, for even though he said he was Daisy's fiancée, she was currently leaning back in the arms of another man who was fondling her naked breasts as she rested her head on his shoulder, her eyes blissfully closed. John scarcely seemed aware of them as he talked with my Master. Apparently, he owned a house in D.C. that boasted a full dungeon, and they (he and Daisy and her nameless paramour, plus a scraggly-looking group of single women) were all going over there now to continue the fun. Upon hearing this, I was filled with despair. All I wanted was to go home and go to bed, and yet for some reason when Master asked me what I thought, I merely shrugged.

Daisy was the one looking smug now as we all walked outside slowly, ostensibly preparing to drive over to John's house. I recognized a single girl in their party as the one who had gone down on Daisy while she was suspended, and another older, rather ugly, woman with kinky blonde hair as the one who had fucked Daisy with a strap-on while she hung in mid-air. Daisy had made so much ecstatic noise during the experience I already knew she and I weren't very much alike, for I could never thrill to the strokes of a dildo like that. Apparently, John had years of experience in the BDSM lifestyle, boasting an unofficial degree in the operation of arcane suspension apparatus. He and Daisy were one of those rare kinky couples also into Swinging, and as we stood outside in the gravel parking lot, she planted herself directly in front of me.

'Mm, what a nice ass,' she said, reaching behind me to squeeze my cheeks. Then my Master stepped up right behind me and she purred, 'Mm, *two* nice asses!' as she pressed hard against me to fondle his tight black leather buttocks.

As everyone prepared to leave in separate cars, I communicated to my Master in a desperate whisper that I had no desire whatsoever to drive to a total stranger's house in the middle of the night. I told him I was tired and wanted to go home. Blessedly patient with me for having failed to clearly communicate this sentiment to him earlier, before he had accepted their invitation, he made an excuse for us (I suggested he tell them we had just returned from Brazil that morning and were suffering from jetlag.) He said we would take a rain check and visit their dungeon another night. The light went out of Daisy's eyes in a way that would have made me feel guilty if I hadn't been so relieved. I was intensely happy to climb back into the jeep where I could relax and stop pretending I had anything in common with those people except the most superficial things. For example, I too owned a black-leather corset my Master had custom ordered for me.

'You know the girl with the short hair, the one wearing the yellow dress?' my Master asked me with a smile a he started the engine.

'What about her?'

'She offered to come over one night and be our slave.'

'She *what*?'

'She offered to come over to our house one night and be our slave.'

'You're kidding me!' I laughed. 'She just came right out and said that?' I was suddenly thinking maybe D.C. wouldn't be so bad after all. In Miami, it had cost me considerable time and effort to drag in the kill of a single girl to feed my Master, and I had only succeeded in doing so once.

'She asked me if we played with girls,' my Master went on, 'and I said we sometimes enjoyed having one over to be our slave for the night.'

I laughed again, pleased to realize I was sincerely feeling more excited by the possibility than jealous. 'Well, she's not all that attractive,' I pointed out cattily. It's a weakness I'm still working on because I've always been very vain of my looks, which has nothing to do with how much I know my Master loves me and how beautiful I am in his eyes.

'She's all right,' he replied more firmly than I liked, but I was too tired to make the mistake of not trusting him again and suffering all the disastrous emotionally exhausting consequences, so I held my tongue... until we got home, then I had a minor nervous breakdown in which I fervently told him there was no way I could stand watching him fuck other women all the time, that once in a while it was exciting, but if it happened regularly it would be intolerable, etc. etc. etc. My poor Master, he was just as tired as I was, yet once again he was forced to summon up the patience and strength to weather a severe emotional storm brought on by lightning flashes of fears that had no place in the loving, trusting, mutually respectful climate of our relationship.

'Missa,' he said quietly, 'I leave it entirely in your hands who we play with and who we don't play with. It's completely up to you. If I put you in charge of this aspect of our life, then maybe you'll stop being so afraid. Maybe it'll help you believe it really *is* all about us and not what you're so afraid it's all about. Do you understand me, Missa?'

'Yes, Master, I think so... thank you, Master.'

'Can we please go to bed now?'

'Yes, Master.'

Excerpts from my Diary:

How far I will go as a slave depends wholly on my Master and the nature of his desires. I trust that body and soul I was made especially for my Master, and that, therefore, whatever it pleases and excites him to demand of me will never be more than I can give.

***

After being flogged at the club, and then fucked violently by my Master, I learned I can take it more deeply and longer and harder than I had believed. The beating opened and softened my cervix up like a flower, so that the next day when the depth and force of his penetrations felt uncomfortable, I let go of the tense fear that they would become even more painful as he pushed my limits. I turned the excruciating sensation of his erection pushing the envelope of my flesh into an intense pleasure that grew and deepened the harder he got and the more violently he thrust.

***

Although there are many things about her and about her relationship with her master that do not personally agree with me, the sentiment Vanessa Duriés expresses here is what every slave who adores her Master feels, 'I offered myself. I spread open like a flower. I was no longer my own master. I belonged to my Master.'

***

As I told my Master, I realized Saturday night at *The Crucible* how much I despise Vanilla Swingers. The idea that I am there to attain mere sexual pleasure with strangers is repellant to me. I would do much better in a BDSM environment where it is obvious and understood that I am there strictly to please my Master, and that doing so is the only pleasure I crave. The knowledge that I am obeying my Master's commands, and fulfilling him by submitting my body to whatever he desires for it, transcends sexual pleasure even while making it mysteriously much more intense. All I want is to be bound and beaten into absolute sensual submission as a physical expression of how much I love my Master, absolutely and unconditionally. My soul worships his being just as all my orifices adore his erection, and open up to whomever he decides may have the pleasure of using what belongs to him. Many Vanilla Swingers – the ones who aren't simply into watching and being watched – are there to satisfy their own selfish lust for physical pleasure with their partner's permission. Where I'm coming from as a beloved and devoted slave is light-years away in another dimension of Swinging altogether.

***

My Master said to me, 'What turns me on about fucking another woman is mainly the fact that you're feeding her to me… it's all mental; fucking other holes isn't pleasurable in itself.'

***

I said to my Master, 'I'm afraid that in the right situations I'll be able to become a slut for you…'

He replied, 'Don't worry, I'm in control. If I ever feel I'm losing control of a situation, I stop it… You have to understand that what excites me is turning you on, Missa; knowing that I'm fulfilling all your fantasies.'

CHAPTER THREE
Dreaming Is Reality

The other night I dreamed I ascended naked into the center of heaven and took control of the atmosphere. Spreading my arms wide, I called colors into life around me, beautiful subtle hues of violet, amethyst and blue. Then the clouds began rising, roiling up towards me a dangerous dark-gold in color, and suddenly I was ecstatically enveloped in a storming ocean of life, my body erotically attacked by every form of being imaginable. Electric eels licked my nipples and twined around me, just one of the infinite creatures pulling me down to earth in the throes of an almost unimaginable pleasure. I remember the smiling face of a dolphin reflecting my pussy's slick pudenda as it swam playfully between my legs, and then I was back on solid ground where my Master was waiting for me and took me in his arms, perfectly completing as well as sheltering me from the world's wild orgy. Then I woke up.

When I say my Master is my dream man, I am not being trite; it's absolutely true. I have spent my whole life dreaming while both awake and asleep, and I've never given up the belief that everything I think and desire plays a vital part in shaping the events of my life and even the people I meet. I don't pretend to understand all the forces at work or what it all means in the end, but I do know for a fact that my attitude is not merely a passive observer. As a little girl, I never once fantasized about a white wedding and a big house full of babies. All I wanted ever since I can remember was to travel to ancient places with my soul mate, and I shocked adults when they asked me what I wanted to write about when I grew up with my reply, 'The metaphysics of sex.' I still feel that way, and in the beginning of my third year with my wonderful Master, I can safely say my dream has come true. And now that it has 'come true' it keeps coming true and becoming truer every day, so a better way to express it is that my dream keeps coming true as the very nature of life itself because I dare to believe it is. I feel as though my Master and I have discovered the entrance to a magnificent temple that's been buried in the sands for centuries, and we're only just beginning to explore with the limited flashlights of our rational minds all the mysteriously beautiful and erotic bas-reliefs carved into the walls and columns leading into a whole new dimension of perception. I've been learning a new way of being ever since I met my Master, and more and more I see the smiling face of the sensually powerful and profoundly wise ancient priestess latent inside me smiling back at me in the mirror.

When I was twenty-two-years-old, I was living in a run-down artist's section of Chicago, dirt-poor by choice and sleeping in a basement. My best friend, Alejandra (whom I fondly called Alley-cat) and I spent our days and nights tripping on acid, smoking pot, listening to music, writing poetry, taking pictures Alley-cat developed in the darkroom behind the curtain hanging next to our bed, and scratching out drawings by candle light. I was determined never to surrender to the nine-to-five death of my soul. We ate potatoes with soft-boiled eggs almost every night and pancake mix from the welfare boxes we picked up. We were perfectly happy. At least we were as happy as we could be while desperately searching for our soul mates. I've kept a journal all my life (collecting dozens of all shapes and sizes rather as I imagine my eternal soul collects lifetimes of experiences) and this an excerpt from the diary I was keeping at the time. For me, reading it now feels like coming across an illuminated manuscript from my own personal dark ages:

I dreamed I was walking through a large deserted parking lot at night. At one end there was an ice cream stand where I bought a chocolate cone. The man gave me ten dollars in change. 'No, that's too much,' I protested. He took it back and handed me a five-dollar bill. It was still too much, but I thrust it into the right pocket of my black jacket feeling it was my reward for being honest the first time, and woke up.

Less than twenty minutes later I was standing in the deserted parking lot of a fast-food restaurant just before sunrise waiting for my friend, Tina, to pick me up. We were driving out to a national park for the day. I was waiting for her red car to pull up and whisk me off into our nature adventure when a handsome black man suddenly approached me.

'Hello,' he said, 'you look sad and lonely standing out here. Do you have a place to stay?'

'Yes, I do,' I replied, 'thank you.'

'You're so thin… are you hungry? Would you like to join me for breakfast?'

'Oh, no, thank you, I'm fine, really.'

'Well, if you ever need anything or just feel like talking, here's my card. Please feel free to call me anytime.'

'Thank you.' I smiled at him.

Suddenly he thrust something into the right pocket of my jacket. 'If you won't have breakfast with me, buy some for yourself,' he said, and walked away.

I put my hand in my pocket and pulled out a five-dollar bill.

I had been wearing the same jacket in the dream in a deserted parking lot, and I suffered the strong sensation that I had somehow brought it with me. I stared at the bill in a shocked daze. Before my sleepy eyes my dream had become reality. 'The Magic Pattern is blatantly telling me something,' I thought. 'It's your dreams that shape reality.' At that moment Tina's red car pulled into the parking lot and I ran towards it grinning with joy.

I never forgot that dream and the lesson it taught me. I slept naked then and I still do, even in the dead of winter; I hate even the slight restriction of a cotton t-shirt becoming tangled around my torso as I toss and turn, buffeted by one dream after another. I never have a problem falling asleep, but I wake up dozens of times every night, which is perhaps one reason why I seem to remember all my dreams – vivid adventures in full living color involving places I've never been before and people I've never met. More than once I've been disappointed to wake up beneath my feather comforter when only an instant before I had been flying over the stunningly beautiful landscape of another planet, for instance. Flying in dreams is an intensely erotic experience for me; gravity ceases to pin me down and instead becomes my partner in an elemental dance, lifting me up and supporting me as I move gracefully and sensually in whichever way I desire. Whatever clothes I'm wearing in the dream invariably get stripped off as I soar towards the earth's atmosphere, until the exquisite moment when it's time to deliberately begin falling, and I am increasingly aroused as the violent moment of contact approaches with whatever lies below me… The landing is always different, but the plunging descent from heaven down to earth is always violent, and the sharper and harder the obstacles in my way, the more intense my sexual arousal becomes as I prepare to collide with them... I long to impale myself on fatally sharp Cathedral spires... I'm desperate to become trapped in the metal web of an unfinished skyscraper... in these dreams every stabbing, crushing object is desirably erotic. My body is a sensually pure, deathless energy aching to be beaten and shaped and used, and I always land in the worst possible public place, for example on dead grass covered with cigarette butts or on black asphalt in the middle of the street at night, utterly exposed and vulnerable to everything and anyone. The other morning when I woke up from one such dream, I was so incredibly turned on, I was more grateful than ever for my Master's miraculous reality as he allowed me to ride his cock, and enjoy two shattering orgasms before he turned me over and gave me a third blinding climax fucking my pussy from behind. The fact that intensely vivid dreams affect my creativity and even my sexuality is one I take totally for granted; it has been 'scientifically' proved in my own life countless times before and continues to be so.

'Magic was not the science of the past. It is the science of the future. I believe that the human mind has reached a point in evolution where it is about to develop new powers – powers that would once have been considered magical. It has always possessed greater powers than we now realise: of telepathy, premonition of danger, second sight... but these were part of its instinctive, animal inheritance. For the past thousand years or so, human-kind has been busy developing another kind of power related to the intellect, and the result is Western civilization. His unconscious powers have not atrophied; but they have gone underground. Now the wheel has come full circle; intellect has reached certain limits, and it cannot advance beyond them until it recovers some of the lost powers... it attempts to make up for lack of broader intuitions with a microscopic attention to detail. It has cut itself off from the source.' [44]

This is what people mean when they talk about returning to a matriarchal society and the rebirth of the goddess. Superficially, the relationship between a Master and his slave appears firmly rooted in the patriarchal – man dominating woman – and I don't argue that the terms 'master' and 'slave' stem from the rational brain; nevertheless, the relationship itself, when deeply lived and practiced, has ancient roots in metaphysics. I think of Stinger as my priest, and everything we do together is a way of worshipping the mystery of our existence, because there's nothing more intensely exciting than embodying cosmic principles in our day-to-day life; an arousing exercise in faith sensually linked with power making us both feel stronger and healthier emotionally and physically. Our loving relationship as Master and slave mysteriously empowers us both. 'And what is, in fact, the source of philosophy – or, for that matter, of any knowledge? It is fundamentally the need for power. You have only to watch the face of a baby who has just learned how to open a door by turning the handle, to understand what knowledge is *for*. In the twentieth century, power has become a suspect word, because it has become associated with the idea of power over other people. But that is its least important application... The power to be derived... is only incidentally a power over things and people. It is basically power over oneself, contact with some "source of power, meaning and purpose" in the subconscious mind.'

My submission to my Master is an act of love, of absolute respect and trust, that blooms naturally inside me, and it is this state of grace (which can be rationally described as a magical perception of existence expressed by way of metaphors) I long to faithfully sustain as a 24/7 slave.

***

'll never forget the morning when my Master said to me from where he still lay in bed, 'If I had my newspaper, I could get up...' Once upon a time, I would have reacted defensively, as though put upon, thinking resentfully, 'As if I don't have enough things to do in the morning!' But I did not feel that way at all; I felt genuine surprise, and a touch of dismay, that I had forgotten my Master's paper. I promptly went to fetch it, as always tempting fate by opening the front door of our apartment completely naked. I hurried back into the bedroom and handed it to him saying, 'I'm sorry, Master, I don't know how I could have forgotten!' The amazing thing is, I wasn't acting; I wasn't forcing myself to behave like a good slave, it was really how I felt. I was reward-ed by my Master abruptly sitting up and hugging me then burying his face in my belly with a hungry, loving growl.

It seems a small incident, but the truth is I crossed a monumen-tal threshold in my psyche that morning that thrills me. Nothing brings me greater happiness than pleasing my Master; nothing. I live in a temple as a priestess-slave devoted to loving and serving the lord of my being. I was placed on this earth for the joy of being myself by fulfilling all his desires. For me happiness and peace and freedom from fears and the tension they breed depend on being as beautiful as possible for my lord and Master. Surrendering posses-sion of my flesh to him transforms it into a sacred vessel, into some-thing so much more... just touching the skin of my inner thighs the other day as I was reading, I experienced a totally fresh sense of wonder at the miracle of my sensuality, which longs to know no bounds in the mysterious life path of fulfilling all my Master's desires, and hence my own.

While idly caressing myself in wonder at the softness of my skin, I was reading Colin Wilson's marvelously comprehensive work, *The*

Occult. 'Why is science so opposed to purpose? Because it has suffered so much from it in the past... The Churchmen who burned Giordano Bruno and made Galileo recant were blocking the progress of science... But while admitting that a non-purposive science may discover many valuable truths, we may still point out that there is no sound scientific reason for actually outlawing the idea of purpose...It is difficult for me not to think of life as process that comes from outside the chemicals involved, and which imposes its own organization on them. There is, as I have already said, an immense difference between an accidental process and a process upon which I concentrate my sense of purpose. There is even an immense difference between doing something absent-mindedly and really concentrating on it. Life is inseparable from the idea of purpose.'

My purpose in life is to be in love with myself and with my Master, which means to be in love with the mystery and sensual beauty of existence and the boundless desire it excites in us for experience. And this purpose is inseparable from why I write. Writing is the unique way I serve in the temple of life and, as I see it, worship the divine purpose behind it, a purpose that is realized precisely through my feelings and perceptions. It's that simple and that infinitely complex for me. I feel blessed to be able to concentrate exclusively on love and creativity – the pulse of my soul – without worrying about my physical existence, which is in my Master's very capable and loving hands. That's not to say I don't make any money, because I do and I always have, but my Master and I support each other one-hundred percent in every sense. I know he'll always take care of me, and he knows I'll always care for him in every conceivable way.

A married couple's life is very often structured by their role as parents. My Master and I have no desire for children. The foundation and organization of our lives is based purely on our metaphysical identities as Master and slave. Our daily life is beautifully organized and intensely punctuated by rituals. I cannot pretend to speak for other Masters and their slaves, but I don't doubt there are men and women out there similar in temperament to Stinger and myself who understand what I'm saying and who, adding their own unique embellishments and modifications, enjoy a similarly structured relationship. There are no Master and slave counselors out there, and I think this is due in great part to the fact that couples in a BDSM relationship tend to be very open and honest with each other about their fears and desires. Holding anything back in a relationship is unhealthy, but in the case of Masters and slaves it can also sometimes be physically dangerous. I have learned to be brutally honest with myself so I may quickly and clearly communicate to my Master what I am feeling and thinking. This is essential since I'm always being gently but relentlessly pushed beyond what I believe to be my limits, but which turn out to be just another threshold it excites me to cross. That's not to say I don't have limits, but they are not determined by my fears and insecurities; they are determined by the nature of my Master's desires. To be soul mates implies that as far as he desires to go is as much as I was made to give.

We recently had drinks with another Master and slave couple, and she and I were both appalled listening to her Master describe some of the slaves he had met in the past who wanted him to participate with them in such incomprehensibly abhorrent activities as mutilation. I enjoyed meeting this couple because she and I were basically on the same wavelength – intelligent and spirited and not at all into extremes of pain. For over a year, I proudly wore the nipple rings my Master gave me before he removed them himself. I had never truly grown accustomed to them; in fact, they were detracting from the sensual pleasure I took in my breasts. Every slave is different. I have very long, thick nipples that are already very sensitive, so that piercing them did not enhance their erotic experience for me, on the contrary. Yet some slaves actually relish the agonizing sensation of having their nipples ripped by piercings, or so I hear; I find it almost impossible to believe. Then again, I've seen photographs of a crucified girl that were undoubtedly real. If Masters and slaves are akin to priests and priestesses, it's not surprising there are those who practice extreme fanatical forms of this almost religiously structured lifestyle. A good, true Master will never push a slave beyond her limits once he has determined them (distinguishing them from her fears and what she only believes to be her limits) and this is something she can count on religiously. She knows the rituals she and her Master perform together will never cross the line where they cease to be pleasurable. She has complete faith in the mysterious fact that she is the embodiment of her Master's desires, and that therefore they will never offend the needs of her own soul, which is mysteriously one with his.

***

As I think I've made clear, one of the most important rituals in a Master and slave relationship is the ritual of discipline. I've discussed how I feel about being spanked… in a sense a good spanking is as much reward as punishment. Discipline is different. There is no pleasure in discipline except for how intense it is, yet as a Sex Slave I worship the pure power of pain and relish the sensation of my body becoming the vessel of its uncompromising power. The experience of pleasure requires at least a modicum of effort. Pain descends like a blessing in that absolutely no effort is required on my part to produce it. Adjectives most often used to describe pain such as 'hot' and 'blinding' also apply to fire – it can be a wonderfully positive tool as well as uncontrollably destructive. My Master carefully controls how much pain he subjects me to when he is disciplining me, and I know I can trust him not to burn down my psychological framework in the process. The pure intensity of pain is sacred when it brings every part of me together in one unarguable, overwhelming experience. My thoughts are no more capable of wrapping themselves around the reality of pain than my fingers are of holding a live flame, yet my body somehow absorbs the searing blow. In that instant of violently forged union between these two parts of me, my soul burns hot and bright – the physical sensation of pain becomes indistinguishable from the emotional sense of how unendurable it would be to continue indulging in whatever fear or weakness prompted the transgression for which I am being punished. My soul is the joy I take in the pain as, by acknowledging my weaknesses, I sense my much deeper strength. My soul thrives in the excruciating throes of knowing that absolute submission to my beloved Master is a haunting form of power much greater than a reasonable tense resistance to it.

Early in our relationship, my Master fashioned a translucent paddle which became the official (and by me much dreaded) instrument of my discipline. This paddle is so hard it cuts right through all the subjective layers of my stubborn indignation and reduces me to a regretful sobbing heap with just one vicious blow across my ass cheeks. There is no arguing with this hand-made paddle when it instantly inscribes a wordless red statement across my outraged buttocks. Whatever thoughts and feelings were disturbing me so much that I misbehaved and displeased my Master are somehow branded into my skin, forcing me to fully face them and deal with them as I might otherwise not have done. Whenever my Master commands me to bend naked over the end of the bed, and I hear him take the paddle down from where it hangs amidst other more sensually enjoyable items, I know I am about to face yet another one of my inner demons in the form of a pain so intense I can either futilely struggle to resist it or transform it into a revelation. After the first blow of the paddle, I am usually sobbing with mingled gratitude for my Master's vigilance, and anger at myself for being so weak and stupid that, yet again, I let myself forget how much he loves me, meaning there's nothing I can't talk to him about rationally and calmly and, above all, respectfully. As long as I am helplessly at the mercy of my fears and insecurities, this translucent paddle will continue to be an instrument of my inner growth wielded by Master's relentlessly loving hand.

At first my Master would decide on the number of blows with the paddle my transgression deserved, and would warn me how many were coming so I could prepare myself for them. Lately, however, he asks me how many blows I feel I deserve, and makes me beg for each one. This slight but vital change in the routine of my discipline tells me how far he thinks I have come, which inspires me to do better, and adds a whole new dimension of effectiveness to my punishments by making me fully responsible for how much I suffer physically as a result of how much I still needlessly allow myself to suffer mentally and emotionally. To an outside observer my transgressions would seem minor, and in the case of 'normal' relationships they might even seem like virtues. A wife has the right to willfully challenge her husband should he interrupt what she is saying and abruptly command her to strip naked and kneel before him, whereas a slave must obey her Master without question. It took me a very long time to obey all of my Master's commands without sometimes whining and complaining even as I reluctantly went through the motions. Then one day it struck me how sloppy I could often be when it came to obeying my Master, and I begged him not to let me get away with it anymore; I asked him to make sure I learned to always obey him instantly and silently no matter what. As a result he was obliged to pull out the translucent paddle more often than I would have believed necessary, and for this I am both ashamed and grateful. It seems the deeper I delve into the mysterious workings of my soul, the more subtle the doubts and fears and psychological obstacles I encounter become. Even as my Master assured me I had made incredible progress and that he was very proud of me, it seemed that nearly every night I found myself bent over the bed, my ass brutally kissed by that paddle over and over again as I kept begging for more punishing strokes. Now I ask for as much as I can take feeling I deserve no less for still being such a sloppy slave after over two years in training. In truth, my Master is more patient with me than I am with myself, and when he takes me in his arms and holds me afterwards, I am crying not because of the physical pain I endured but because of the psychic misery it causes me to doubt him and hence to challenge his commands.

Paradoxically, the better a slave I become, the more I feel just the slightest transgression – for example raising my voice to my Master and using a less than respectful tone when talking to him about something – deserves to be severely punished. It's like tuning a fine instrument learning to play the beautifully complex melody of submission in a perfect harmony of love and respect.

There's an old Celtic saying, 'He who exposes himself to the dangers of the sword-edge bridge places himself within reach of salvation.' A Master and his beloved slave dare to walk the 'sword-edge' bridge together in that there would seem to be a dangerously fine line between controlled discipline and physical abuse, but the truth is that being spanked, paddled or flogged as a slave bears absolutely no relationship whatsoever to abusive acts that fall under the heading of 'domestic violence'. When a dancer works with a choreographer she/he is willing to suffer physically for the sake of the pleasure and fulfillment they take in embodying a vision of beauty and sensuality that cannot be reached without effort, dedication, and the willingness to push muscles beyond their normally prescribed limits. For me being a Sex Slave is very much like being a dancer forever in training. My Master and I have a vision of what a truly beautiful and sensual relationship between a man and a woman should be like, and to that end I willingly obey the demands of a profoundly challenging erotic choreography that brings out the best in me while realizing all his dreams and desires. It's true I have had to train many of my psychological muscles to work in a whole new way, and I am constantly having to 'stretch' how I perceive certain actions and how I feel about them, but the result is the pleasure of dancing – of living – as gracefully and intensely as possible without constantly stumbling over fears and frustrations that have no place on the stage of a truly fulfilling relationship.

A slave needs her Master to train her like dancers and athletes need a coach who will push them beyond what they might feel are their natural limits. A lazy recalcitrant athlete might be punished with four extra laps around the track, and as a slave I often ask my Master to give me four extra smacks of the paddle whenever he is rightfully punishing me for what I have come to think of as an inexcusable laziness on my part. I have the ability to be a graceful slave 24/7 and to fully enjoy the kinky *pas de deux* my Master and I have chosen for ourselves, and even though it is natural to stumble in life, and to be tired and need to rest, there is no excuse for constantly questioning the mysterious rightness of my chosen choreography.

Being a beloved Sex Slave is like being a prima ballerina and nothing like being an abused wife or girlfriend, yet accidents can happen, which is why Masters and slaves are walking 'the sword-edge bridge' where their agreed upon Safe Word is a vital safety net over the power of the subconscious to temporarily yet completely drown the rational mind. I mentioned the interminable relationship I endured with my living Ken doll… this relationship was punctuated by isolated moments of extreme violence that weren't overtly directed at me until the end, when I promptly left him. He would suffer occasional fits during which he broke things, and once he even put his fist through a window, shattering it, before he punched the glass over a painting and broke his hand. As a result, broken glass and hostile violence are inextricably linked in my emotional synapses, so that one night when my Master accidentally knocked over the glass covering of an oil lamp when he swung his arm to spank me, I reacted with a blind fear to the sound of glass shattering that made a usually enjoyable act of punishment suddenly feel like abuse. Instead of feeling his love for me in the exercise of discipline, I felt as though he was angry with me. It was a terrible experience, yet it only lasted a few seconds as my Master quickly realized there was something wrong, at which point he took me tenderly in his arms, and held me there firmly for a long time as he untangled the psychological knot behind my reaction.

There is nothing on this earth like the depth and strength of the tenderness in which my Master enfolds me when I am reduced to a trembling pulp of raw emotions all having their way with me until I can think clearly again and, with his infinitely patient help, straighten them out. That night I quickly ran the gamut of reactions from blind fear to defensive anger to miserable unhappiness to sobbing relief to a sniffling numbness gradually becoming a grateful sense of peace as I watched my Master cleaning up the glass shards strewn across the area rug and carpet. When I made to help, he gently commanded me to stay where I was on my slave pillow, and the vital differences between Stinger's soul and the infinitely inferior personality of the man whose actions had left me emotionally scarred were all healingly reinforced inside me as I watched him remove the rug, shake the glass out over the balcony railing outside, and then vacuum the carpet thoroughly, after which he replaced the rug and put the sweeper away. (When I next used it, I marveled at how neatly he had folded the electrical chord, much more patiently than I ever do.)

Such moments may be frightening and painful, but they are also intensely cathartic. This particular incident has greatly reduced the power of broken glass to shatter me to pieces inside. Other slaves understand these moments of blind emotional reactions, and when they cannot be immediately overcome is when our Safe Word rescues us from the drowning depths of our subconscious. The few times I have used my Safe Word whatever issue prompted it was immediately set aside by my Master for us to discuss either then or later. During our first two years together, my emotional wiring sometimes felt like a hopeless tangle stretching all the way back to my childhood, and there's still no telling when I'll blow a mysterious fuse and, for some reason or other, find one of my Master's commands impossible to obey. I am happy to say that such short-circuits occur less and less frequently, although when they do they can be severe and spark all sorts of insecurities I didn't even realize were there. But after two years, my psyche feels much more fire-proof than it ever did before as the deepest, darkest aspects of my personality continue to be illuminated by the light of my Master's love.

CHAPTER FOUR
A Dungeon In The Attic

We received an e-mail from John and Daisy, the couple we had met at the crucible. The subject line read, *Hello Beautiful Missa and Sexy Stinger*, which spoke well for their powers of perception, and one evening we drove over to their house in D.C. Master and I were excited about experiencing a real-live dungeon, and this couple intrigued us as one of the few we had met who crossed the line between Swinging and BDSM. I was not in the least bit attracted to John (in fact, there was something about him that repelled me) and my Master assured me that, as always, he would take my feelings into consideration. At this point in our relationship we had not yet clearly defined our Swinging parameters in a way I felt completely comfortable with, so naturally I was tense on the drive over. I was wearing an over-sized Betty Page T-shirt over my favorite clingy mini-dress – the black one that sparkles like the night sky full of stars – white-and-clear extreme high-heels with matching glitter on the straps, and nothing else. My scant attire made me even more nervous as we found ourselves in a rather questionable neighborhood crowded with cars and lined with run-down looking three-story townhouses. As the Brits say, I was more nervous than two very nervous things, and there's an odd metaphysical accuracy to this expression for in a sense I was two people as I stepped carefully out of the jeep onto the street. I was Missa, aroused by the challenge of sensually submitting to her beautiful Master's desires in the inspiring setting of a genuine dungeon. And I was MIP, questioning the wisdom and desirability of driving to a complete stranger's house to 'play' in a rather iffy neighborhood simply because they owned a dungeon. I was in truth beside myself with anxiety, but fortunately both of me were absolutely in love with Stinger and trusted him to take care of us, so I was able to assume a semblance of calm...

Until John answered the door, then my heart plummeted, and it had a long way to go perched as I was on five-inch heels. Daisy's master looked even scankier in broad daylight than I remembered. I glanced up into my Master's eyes as we stepped inside, silently but quite fervently communicating to him the words, 'There's no way in hell I'm sleeping with this guy!' I am my Master's slave and must do whatever he says, which makes it imperative for me to communicate my thoughts and feelings to him, because he loves me and therefore will never command me to do anything he knows will really hurt me physically or emotionally. He is wise enough to distinguish between skittishness on my part and my soul's absolute refusal to sink so low. As we walked down the dim corridor he squeezed my hand and looked down into my eyes in a very reassuring way, and I desperately needed the sense of his strength and protection because the run-down quality of the place was already depressing me.

'Daisy's upstairs getting ready,' John informed us, preceding us into a medium-sized kitchen that like the rest of the place looked relatively clean but ragged around the edges. This was explained when we started talking and he informed us he was a contractor about to undertake the massive task of fixing up the place. Two dogs the size of small horses sauntered into the kitchen, and I relieved a small amount of my tension petting them. At last Daisy appeared, and my heart squirmed somewhere between my heels where it had become caught when John opened the door; I felt as though I was stepping all over it when I greeted her cheerfully, pressing her naked bosom against me. I have been accused both of vanity and of having a low self-esteem as far as my body image is concerned, and both are probably true in different moments. That evening I was at once proud of my pert breasts, tight aureoles and long sensitive nipples, as well as a bit jealous of Daisy's much bigger tits where they hung out of the topless corset she was wearing over a mini skirt, and heels that were nowhere near as high as mine. My Master was in his black leather pants and boots, and he looked like a veritable prince of the blood beside David, who was not as tall and bordered on thin in his casual black T-shirt and jeans.

We made conversation in the kitchen then carried our drinks into a dark living room half consumed by two massive dog pillows. Happily there was also a couch for us humans, and I was delighted to see two large platters of cheese, crackers and fruit laid out for us and offering a welcome buffer between the safe, socially polite present and less palatable intimate activities later in the evening. I sat down next to my Master, and John took the master's chair with Daisy perched on his knees. The conversation ranged from the benefits of the Atkins Diet, which they were both following, to the joy of playing with needles. I concentrated on deliciously chewy morsels of cheese to stay calm, for John was entertaining the fantasy of introducing me to the orgasmic potentials of piercing which had as much chance of coming true as the couch Master and I were sitting on flying to the moon.

'How do you know you wouldn't be into it?' John insisted with his matter-of-fact politeness that barely concealed an arrogance he obviously felt was justified by his years of experience.

'Because I know!' I had already told him about my pierced nipples and how little they had agreed with me. 'I'm not nineteen-years-old anymore,' I added. 'I'm a grown woman and I've had time and experiences to help me determine what I am and am not into.' Not to mention the fact that, in my opinion, the pain of needles stabbing through my nipples was one I had to be insane to want to experience again.

'You've just never tried it,' he went on obstinately. 'You should-n't close yourself to new experiences...' And he went on and on to describe Daisy's ecstatic experiences with needles and other activities, including fire and breath-play.

I kept glancing at my Master wondering how he could be so calm and relaxed in the face of the increasingly disturbing scenarios painted by our host, who did not shy away from boasting about his years of experience in the BDSM scene. We learned he had regularly dominated both men and women, a fact that turned me off even more, if possible. In contrast to her master and husband (they were newlyweds) Daisy was a delight – cheerful, sympathetic to my feelings and limits, and a wonderfully energetic hostess, making sure our glasses were always filled. And because I liked her so much, it was even harder for me to watch as John bound her arms behind her back, and then put her breasts in bondage using a contraption resembling a crossbow armed with clothespins that tightened their cruel grip on her nipples whenever he turned a small lever. And he turned that evil lever a lot, causing Daisy's initial smiling compli-ance to become more and more strained where she perched on his knees, until I saw her whisper something in his ear and knew she was begging him to release her because she couldn't bear the pain much longer.

'Why are you doing this to her?' I demanded of John.

'Because I can,' he replied smugly.

'He's enjoying the power he has to make you feel uncomfortable, Missa,' my Master explained, in my opinion a despicable reason to make a women suffer such torment as I can only imagine those clothespins caused her. I cannot tolerate any sort of clamp on my nipples; I cannot fathom how she endured it.

'Would you like me to release her?' John asked me.

'Yes, please!'

He did so at last, and the mute relief in Daisy's lovely eyes prompted me to put down my wineglass and ask her sadistic master, 'May I kiss them to make them feel better?'

'Yes, you may,' he replied, a glint of surprise in his eyes as I stood up and gently cupped Daisy's soft, slack bosom in my hands, bending over to lightly kiss both her nipples. 'Does that feel better?' I asked.

'Oh, yes, Missa,' she answered, smiling with pleasure. 'Thank you, Missa.'

I sat back down again next to my Master, who caressed me approvingly.

'I love the way her skirt just barely covers her ass,' John remarked, referring to the cut of my starry dress, and things felt a little better for a while, until he began talking about a set of prize silver surgical tools he inherited from a friend who, before he died of AIDS, enjoyed letting John torture his urethra with them.

'Excuse me, did you say his *urethra*?' I asked in stupefaction.

'Yes,' John's eyes glowed with dark satisfaction as he absorbed my shock. 'How would you feel about helping me give them a demonstration, Daisy?'

She was either a doormat or incredibly brave or both. I clearly discerned the subliminal tensing of her body even as she responded, 'I'll try anything once' or something to that inane effect, and he promptly ordered her to go start boiling the instruments in their special pressure cooker.

I looked at my Master. His utterly mild demeanor in the face of such an abhorrent – totally not erotic or arousing – activity frightened and infuriated me at the same time. I slid away from him on the couch to let him know I was having a serious problem with the proceedings, but he merely smiled calmly at me. I think it was at that point, while his surgical tools were being sterilized, that John asked us about our Swinging etiquette with all the passion of a surgeon preparing to operate on me.

'Missa has certain rules she has to obey,' my Master informed him in that calm, quiet voice of his that somehow manages to convey infinite authority, 'and one of them is that she's not allowed to taste another man's bodily juices.' He was coolly telling John I would never suck his cock unless he wore a condom, which it later turned out he would not, not even for penetration. He protested that it ruined the experience for him, which of course meant he wasn't coming anywhere near me.

Fortunately, we finally went upstairs to see the dungeon, which was actually in the attic, and the surgical tools sterilizing in the pressure cooker were forgotten; I never had to endure the agonizing sight of John inserting them into Daisy's urethra. I liked her very much as a person, yet it was slaves like her – who will endure essentially anything to please their sadistic masters – that frightened me away from the lifestyle in the first place.

John's attic was a true party room and, thanks in great part to Daisy (who knew exactly where to find everything when John asked for it) very well organized. Their attic playroom was equipped with just about everything you could possibly need and desire; there was even a small water cooler in a corner where the ceiling sloped to meet the floor. It was a spacious attic, and Master and I exclaimed over it in unfeigned admiration. Yet it was missing the Gothic atmosphere of a dungeon and therefore lacked some ineffable but vital quality that was only somewhat made up for by the triangular ceiling. There was a sex swing, a leather 'chair' equipped with shackles, a large mattress in the corner covered with what Daisy assured me were fresh sheets, other assorted toys and their containers, and pillows were strewn across the carpet. My Master and I settled back against some, contentedly sipping our drinks. I was on my second Vodka on ice, and when John offered me two mild painkillers to go with it, I hesitated only a moment before accepting them. Very soon I was feeling no pain, and because a full swap was almost certainly out of the question due to insurmountable safe-sex issues, I found myself feeling completely relaxed.

Inevitably, Daisy and I ended up fooling around while our Master's watched. We kissed and caressed, and she pulled my dress down to expose my breasts so we could both fondle each others very different bosoms. It was a pleasant activity, and my Master's broad smile told me I was pleasing him.

'You know, I've seen this hundreds of times,' John mused, 'but for some reason, I'm getting realty turned on right now…'

'He has an ashtray with your picture on it,' Daisy informed me. 'Has anyone ever told you you like a lot like Petty Page?'

'Yes.' In fact, I'm told that with some frequency, yet it's always nice to hear it. 'I have to pee,' I announced, preparing to make my torturous way down the steep flight of steps to the downstairs bathroom. A convenient chamber pot was the only thing missing in that attic, but it turns out I didn't need one after all.

'Oh, master, can I let her pee on me?' Daisy pleaded.

'Sure,' he said, and my Master's smile deepened as he slipped our credit-card sized digital camera out of his leather pants preparing to document the event.

Daisy and John efficiently prepared the section of floor space available for the 'ceremony' by spreading a large plastic bag over the carpet and covering part of it with a white bed sheet. He then helped her out of her tight bodice so she could spread herself naked across it.

Stinger asked, 'Are you ready, Missa?'

'Yes, Master.' I smiled at him, amused by the proceedings. 'I've never peed on anyone before in my life,' I said as I dug my high-heels into the floor on either side of Daisy's hips, and lifted my little sparkling dress up around my waist. Naturally, I wasn't wearing any panties. I bent my knees slightly, planted two fingertips just above my urethra, and enjoyed a strangely sweet revenge by peeing all over the slave of the man who had dared to even think about torturing this part of my body. My Master had instructed me to practice aiming my urine, and my sessions in the bathtub paid off that night as I aimed the flow of my golden rain across Daisy's belly and breasts, even going so far as to wet her neck just below the chin. I had drunk a considerable amount of Vodka mixed with ice; the sheet was drenched by the time I finished, and my Master had had time to photograph the scene from every angle.

'Mm, you taste so good!' Daisy moaned, licking her lips on which a few stray drops of my piss had apparently landed.

'Very good, Missa,' Master praised me as we sat down and he handed me back my drink.

'Did you enjoy that?' I asked him.

'Very much.'

I couldn't understand why, but I was feeling too good to care. Then I heard Daisy whisper to John as they were cleaning up, 'It tasted so good, so clean… I've never tasted such sweet piss before. Next time, master, can I swallow it?'

'No, of course not!' he snapped. 'That's disgusting!'

I smiled up into my Master's eyes. John had proudly described to us how Daisy had swallowed all his piss when they were lying in bed together that afternoon so he wouldn't have to get up. 'It's an act of love' he had said. No wonder he was jealous of her desire to swallow my urine. But I'll return to the subject of 'Golden Rain' later…

The rest of the evening flowed smoothly and rather enjoyably. Eventually, both men pulled their cocks out of their pants, and I hungrily swallowed my Master's erection while Daisy went down on John. It was when we were all relaxing again sipping our drinks that Daisy suddenly pounced on my Master's lap and started sucking him for all she was worth, slurping noisily up and down his shaft as he and I smiled into each other's eyes. Later Master said to me, 'When she was sucking my dick you just looked totally happy' and I was; I was delighted to relax and watch a lovely little slave slut passionately serving my beautiful Master.

'I didn't give you permission to do that,' John stated quietly, and Daisy sat bolt upright, for all the world like an eager puppy who hadn't even thought of resisting the deliciously big bone in front of her. 'If this were just a normal swinging situation I wouldn't have minded,' he explained mildly, 'but we're with another Master and slave tonight, and you need to have my permission before you do things like that.'

'Yes, master, I'm sorry,' she murmured, and proceeded to apologize to him by fervently sucking his cock again, at which point my Master positioned me on my hands and knees and began fucking me from behind. But I wasn't facing anything interesting, so I gradually turned in the direction of Daisy's buttocks, which loomed enticingly close to my face. For a minute or two I resisted, but then I couldn't help myself, I just had to spread her thighs and tease her pussy with the tip of my tongue, before I dared moving my mouth up to the prize I really craved and began licking her ass, strangely blinded by hunger for it. I could tell from the force of his thrusts that my Master was both surprised and pleased by my initiative, and I heard Daisy whisper to John, 'Yes, she licked my pussy and now she's licking my ass...' I could have rimmed her for a long time while my Master fucked me, but suddenly she turned around, and Stinger pulled out of me obligingly so she could push me onto my back and go down on me. I have a feeling she was very good at it, but I didn't feel anything worth mentioning, so after a moment I gently took hold of her head, and with an apologetic smile urged her to stop wasting her time. The wounded look in her eyes took me by surprise, and I felt bad when she went and knelt in a corner, looking deeply upset by my rejection.

'Come here...' I urged, and made her take my place on her back. I glanced up at my Master to make sure he appreciated what I was about to do, and I'm sure at the time he believed I was doing it mainly to please him, but the truth is I *wanted* to lick this girl's pussy. Then I lost sight of him as I lowered my head between her thighs, tossing my long dark hair back over my shoulders so the men could watch as I tongued her cunt. I was amazed by how much I enjoyed burying my face in another woman's sex, and was equally surprised by her cries of pleasure, which seemed to indicate I knew what I was doing. And I felt as though I did, the tip of my tongue a quivering antenna sensitive to her slightest reaction. For the first time since Master and I embarked on our exciting erotic adventures, I was licking pussy not to please him but because I actually wanted to.

'Did you like that?' I asked her, bemused by my instinctive skill, not quite convinced she hadn't been acting. I had to take her word for it, but then all thoughts of her pleasure were driven out of me as Master urged me onto the swing. Standing in front of me, he raised my legs up around him and penetrated me. John watched him fucking me while Daisy disappeared to use the bathroom, and even though I didn't like him, it turned me on to hold another man's eyes while Master banged me.

When Daisy returned, she asked me if there was any fantasy of mine she could help fulfill, and I admitted to wanting to experience a three-way penetration. She was more than willing to pull out a strap-on and make my dream come true, but John (it seemed to me resentful of the fact that I would not suck his cock without protection) refused to cooperate. He wasn't in the mood and he didn't really want to wear a condom, which 86'd that fantasy fast; however, it left another one intact, and I selected a big black dildo from their collection Daisy eagerly attached to her strap-on. We then moved over to the mattress in the corner, and while John watched, his slave spread herself on her back, I straddled the big lubricated penis she was sporting, slowly burying it in my pussy as Master knelt behind me. Sometimes when he pushes his hard-on into my anus my sphincter resists; it hurts and I have to make an effort to relax. That night – thanks to a combination of Vodka and painkillers, just the right quality of erotic foreplay, and how much I liked the eager smiling girl beneath me – my Master's erection thrust into my ass almost effortlessly. I was a little too high to remember the experience clearly, but I do know I thoroughly enjoyed it. My cunt and my butt were both gloriously filled up, and it was almost more than I could stand and just enough to overwhelm me with a violently profound pleasure. I alternated between arching my spine to press back against my beloved Master as he reamed me in rhythm with my hips riding the black dildo stretching open my pussy, and falling against the delicious contrast of Daisy's soft skin and yielding breasts, kissing her in gasping gratitude for the experience. My Master came inside me just in time; just when I couldn't take much more of the extreme, all-consuming fulfillment, and the feel of his cock pulsing in my ass as his hot spunk shot deep into my body was exquisitely magnified by the black rod stretching my pussy open and making my backdoor even tighter than normal.

That was a very nice end to a night that had its pleasurable moments, and as we said our goodbyes, I was already wondering if it would be possible for Master and me to have Daisy all to ourselves sometime…

* * *

I finished writing *The Story of M – A Memoir* and suffered the odd experience of being forced to answer a series of questions posed to me by a publicist hired to promote the book. She and I talked for over an hour on the phone, reinforcing what I already knew – that I am much better at writing about my feelings. She put together a Press Release that included a description of the book, an author's bio, and a very brief Q&A session:

Born in Cuba, Maria moved to Miami when she was ten months old, and two years later moved to northern Virginia, when her father began work with USAID. When she was 17, her family returned to Miami, where Maria finished high school. She then attended Florida International University. She says, "Because I was raised in Virginia, I consider myself an American. I didn't grow up in Miami, so I never had the full Cuban-American exile experience. I think and dream and write in English." Both her parents now live apart in Miami, and Maria resides in the Northeast after living in Chicago, London, Boston, Atlanta and Miami.

Ever since she was six years old, Maria has been writing. She loved Nancy Drew books when she was young, but began devouring the classics, beginning with Tolstoy, at age twelve. She was also fascinated with the ancient Egyptian culture from a very early age. In her early twenties, she self-published a book of poems, *Fragments For A Papyrus*, and continued to write poetry for several years. Maria then began to publish in literary journals. The first of these were science fiction and fantasy stories, one of which won second place in the New England Association for Science Fiction Fantasy.

Until recently, Maria worked part-time office jobs "in order to have the time and energy to write, which is what I love to do and absolutely have to do to be truly happy." She then became an editor for her U.K. publisher, Chimera Publishing, Ltd. At the publisher's suggestion to "stop holding yourself back and write what you really feel and want to write," Maria began to write erotica.

Q: Why did you decide to write *The Story of M...A Memoir*?

A: I wanted to tell the truth about a loving bondage and domination (BDSM) relationship, that women don't have to lose their personalities as one half of a master-slave couple. There are too many stereotypes in circulation. I wanted to break those stereotypes with an honest, intelligent account of a couple truly in love and say, "This is what we do." Plus I wanted women to know it's okay to explore their darker fantasies, that you don't have to be afraid to explore your sexuality.

Q: In your book, you say you're not a feminist but very independent. What did you mean by that?

A: I like an independent lifestyle; I didn't want to be beholden to any one group or political faction. I don't want men telling me what to do, and I don't want women telling me what to wear or how to express myself. I love men, and I wanted to be able to pursue my interests independently.

Q: What does the word slave mean to you?

A: To me the word *slave* has no more negative connotations than the word spirit.

Q: You were born in Cuba and grew up in the U.S., yet you consider yourself an American. Did you ever feel connected to the U.S. Cuban exile community?

A: No, because I really grew up in northern Virginia when my father worked with USAID. It wasn't until I was 17 that my family moved back to Miami, so as far as I was concerned, I was American through and through. I speak and write and dream in English, not Spanish, so that affects my sense of myself too.

Q: How do you define femininity?

A: Femininity is receptive and yielding and giving and strong all at the same time. I believe femininity should be conscious of itself and not divorced from other parts of a person, male or female. Real femininity is about real strength.

I dreaded the possibility of being constantly interviewed about my feelings – it felt like willingly offering myself up for a living autopsy. I could just feel the cold scalpel of question after question slicing into my chest and hands pulling my heart out to analyze it as mysterious punishment for daring to beat so unconventionally. I needn't have worried; I've gotten much more positive feedback on The Story of M than negative, perhaps because those readers attracted to the book in the first place were ready to hear what I had to say. If my struggles with the lifestyle can help other women make sense of their own experiences, then I'm happy. My sister, Lourdes Maria, was one of the first people to read the book, and she wrote me an e-mail I dreaded would be a typical reaction to my book from women. Fortunately, that hasn't been the case, but I'm sure many women might feel this way:

Yes, I agree to a point. But there is a big difference between a codependent relationship and an interdependent one. Aside from all the sexual exploration and openness you have in your relationship which I would never in a million years ever want for me, your relationship reminds me way too much of the patriarchal model that has held woman back for centuries. To worship another human being 24/7 and be their 'slave' in everyway 24/7 is not an interdependent model of a relationship. To me the master / slave thing is only for fun and only in the bedroom. With a little spanking at most! Anyway, if you are really going to live the way women have been forced to live for a long time, but you willingly do it, then I think the fact that you are not married to him is complete bullshit. You need to re-evaluate why you don't want the marriage thing with him. You need to protect yourself, because, like with any job you would hope there is a good retirement package when it ends. Nothing lasts forever, because there is that possibility down the road even if you don't break up, death happens to us all. So consider marrying him and that way you have his real devotion and respect. Anything less is undermining your full time job frankly. You get what I am saying? I know you said you don't want to be his third wife but the fact of the matter is until you walk down the isle with this man I am not convinced he feels that love you talk about. Because it's too one sided to begin with. You should abandon your fear of marriage and open yourself up to that the same way you open yourself up to everything else with him. Not that I am in general a big believer in it, but in this case I believe it's the right thing to do! For what its worth.

To which I replied:

That Stinger truly loves me and I truly love him is an unquestionable fact no matter what you or anyone else might think about it. There's no earthly need whatsoever to succumb to the social convention of marriage to take care of each other. I'm disappointed you didn't see that the moral of the story is - Stinger takes care of me and I take care of him in ways that suit us both perfectly. Think of it as two kids who are best friends for life playing a game they're really into. That's what it's like, and it's great…

And yet I couldn't help it… part of me felt the same way about marriage deep-down despite all the best efforts I made to talk myself out of it.

Q: You've said that "faith and marriage have degenerated into empty symbols." Do you still believe in marriage?
A: I don't believe or disbelieve in marriage as an institution. If that's what people want, then fine. I do think marriage has lost some of its sacred nature.

Q: Do you want to get married to your master, Stinger?
A: I don't care if I get married because I can still live with the person I love. I never had fantasies about a white wedding and I never wanted children. For me it's more pure for us to live together. There's no external force binding us. We're together only because we want to be.

I did not for one second buy into the conventional feminine perspective that if a man doesn't marry you he doesn't really love you, which was right up there with all the trite beliefs I had already chewed on until I was sick to my soul and finally spit out, for example, a man who truly loves you will not share you with another man. It's frightening the power such trite moral slogans have on our lives. And yet the issue of marriage kept eating away at the edges of my psyche, even after Master and I talked about it and he said he would be happy to draw up legal papers to protect me in case something happened to him, and vise versa. If the obsession with marriage in a woman's make-up was a socially bred instinct born of the need for self-preservation – notice my sister referring to a relationship as a full-time job with the need for accident and life insurance, and there is no doubt in my mind that is one of the principal reason many women want to get married – then when Stinger and I signed legal documents granting me the same legal benefits as a wife, I should have been satisfied... but I wasn't. Whether I admitted it or not, it really bothered me that Daisy and John were married and my Master and I weren't. Deep inside me there was a little Catholic school girl hugging her knees to her chest and pouting and crying because she was denied the ultimate proof of love even though she knew perfectly well the love was there and real and forever.

The subtle but vital torment caused me by the issue of marriage affected me like a profound toothache, making me subconsciously tense, and it all came to a head one night when I responded to one of Master's command's with a hostility that was totally uncalled for and seemed to come out of nowhere for no reason. Have I mentioned that all the pain I have suffered since I met Stinger is a result of my underestimating him and assuming I knew what he was thinking, erroneously projecting my own fears onto his motivations? Yes, well, all this time I had been assuming marriage was out of the question between us; that we had chosen the roles of Master and slave not husband and wife, and that the twain would never meet. It took a severe flogging as punishment for what Master rightly perceived as inexcusable insubordination on my part to wring the confession out of me that I simply couldn't understand why, if we loved each other so much, we couldn't get married.

'I know it's not necessary, I know you love me!' I sobbed. 'I know you'll take care of me and that you've had bad experiences with marriage, but… but I also don't see why we can't ever get married! I know it doesn't prove anything, but it wouldn't hurt us either, would it? I mean…'

'Missa, what's important is us, not the roles Master and slave or husband and wife. It's not only possible, in fact, it's highly probable we'll get married one day.'

I love the statue of St. Theresa writhing in ecstasy beneath the handsome young angel preparing to pierce her heart with a divine arrow. That night kneeling at my Master's feet with my tear-streaked face lying in his lap, the arrow found it's mark – a happiness, a pure joy such as I had never known, suffused my entire being. *I* was the one who had been limiting our relationship. *I* was the one who erroneously believed our love was limited to certain labels, which was a perverse form of reverse conventionalism.

Stinger and I love each other and our love is not defined or confined by either conventional or unconventional roles, and yet avoiding the concept of marriage would have given it a negative power over us, whereas in reality our love is more than deep enough to encompass it. I was a Catholic school girl weeping and trembling with relief in daddy's arms as he pulled her up onto his lap and gave her what she desperately wanted.

'There are no limits to our love, Missa,' he murmured. 'Why did you think it wasn't possible we would get married one day?'

I couldn't speak; I was crying too hard.

'Answer, me, Missa, why did you believe we would never get married?'

'I don't know!' I sobbed. 'I thought… I thought you didn't want to spoil what we had… that marriage makes things different and… and we chose to be Master and slave not husband and wife… and… I don't know! I just thought you didn't want that because it would somehow ruin things between us…'

'The only thing that can ruin anything between us is your being afraid to trust me. Do you trust me, Missa? Do you trust I'm telling you the truth when I say I love you more than anything, that you're the most important thing in my life and all that really matters is our love for each other?

'Yes, Master!'

'There aren't any rules we have to follow, Missa. Our relationship is based on promises, not rules, and I promise you, once we know where I'll be working after this and we can buy a house we'll get married, hopefully sooner than later.'

CHAPTER FIVE
Promises Not Rules

One morning when we were driving to an outlet mall to meet his parents for the day, Master asked me to describe to him one of my sexual fantasies. I found myself at a complete loss, and after a long silence concluded, 'My fantasy is to fulfill all our sexual fantasies, Master.' It was true; all my sexual fantasies had become firmly rooted in reality. It was an exciting realization, and I basked in the heady atmosphere of his approval as he smiled at me and squeezed my knee. If Stinger and I have done anything together since we met it's explore all our sensual fantasies, and we have learned vital things about each other actually sharing experiences that for many people remain only wistful erotic dreams. For over two years I struggled to believe that being fucked by two, or even three, men at the same time was still one of my pet fantasies; however, the truth was I now only desired my Master and that fantasy had mysteriously evaporated like steam over the intense emotional and sexual frustration I lived with for so long in the wrong relationship. Yet I believed that as a slave one of the 'rules' I was 'forced' to obey was submissively suffering other men's cocks inside me for my Master's pleasure in showing me off, and in fully possessing me by sharing me as he enjoyed me from different perspectives. I thought this 'rule' would always be part of our desire to take our intimacy to the deepest levels possible. I believed this 'rule' was set in stone, and that for the rest of my life I would have to live with the thought of periodically watching my Master fuck some fortunate woman while I suffered another lesser man inside me.

As is evidenced in *The Story of M*, playing with another couple was always extremely difficult for me and inevitably much more painful than fulfilling, even when I finally realized my pet fantasy of a double penetration with my Master's cock in my pussy and another man's hard-on in my ass. That was the fantasy; in reality I didn't really enjoy it all that much. Then we played alone with a single girl in our home and I loved every second of it, except for brief stabs of jealousy I was rewarded for controlling by a truly fulfilling evening. There was a lesson to be learned in how much I enjoyed that experience compared to a full swap with a couple, but I was still too proud, and too adamantly not bisexual, to grasp it. I kept thinking that if Stinger was sometimes going to fuck other women, then it was only fair I get to fuck other men, and I spent a great deal of time conceptualizing this stance. I had begun working on a second erotic romance for Magic Carpet I had actually written years ago and was merely adding graphic sex scenes to. The plot was a fantastic metaphysical justification for my pet fantasy of being possessed by three men at once. It involves a Druid high priest – the man the heroine truly loves and desires – and two other equally attractive virile men embodying the forces of light and dark, life and death. In this conversation with the high priest, the conflict I felt in loving Stinger and wanting only him yet also sometimes fucking other men is obvious:

From *Pleasures Unknown:*

Turning towards her, he idly played with one of her star-shaped earrings again. 'I'm challenging you, not hurting you, Maia. You said you would do anything I told you to.'

She could only look beseechingly up into his eyes attempting to brace herself for his departure feeling like someone lost in deep space storing up enough oxygen to survive until she could safely dock with her ship again.

'Slip that tight moral leash off your inner wolf, Maia and spend some time with it,' he commanded quietly. 'Throw your wolf some raw flesh that hasn't been properly prepared for you over a romantic flame. Don't be afraid to surrender to lust and to just enjoy what your body has to offer without worrying about the consequences and your so-called meaningful long-term relationship with Chris. If you can't do this for me, then you can't be my priestess.'

'If discarding my moral sense is part of preparing myself to be the priestess of your so-called religion, then it's the devil you worship,' she accused him listlessly. 'I can't separate sex from love. I have no desire to.'

'Don't be a fool,' he said shortly, and she became aware of several people watching them as he slipped an arm around her waist while his other hand cradled the back of her head. 'You'll do as I say, Maia. Understand me?'

She closed her eyes. 'Yes, Drew.'

'Trust me this is for your own good.'

'I do trust you, Drew, I don't know why, but I do.' She felt irrationally humiliated by a sudden burst of laughter nearby just as she opened her eyes again and let her soul dive up into his unfathomable blue irises. 'Please tell me you're real and not like all these other people here, Drew, I mean truly real.'

'I'm real, Maia,' he caressed the back of her head gently, 'and I know that one of the hardest things in life is not belonging to a tradition and longing to fit into one. It took me a long time, but I finally realized the answer was not trying to belong anywhere anymore but just being myself. The only problem is new ideas and ways of being don't come with maps and safe comfortable little arrows pointing you in absolutely the right direction, it's the price you pay when you're forging your own way through life. You find yourself trying to unite paths that have been unnaturally split, forks in the road that lead to dead ends if you choose one over the other, which is why the devil carries a pitchfork, because evil lies precisely in this unnatural division. The truth is that your spirituality and your sensuality work together like your lovely legs, Maia, and tonight I want you to spread them wide for me. I want you to think about me while Eric is fucking you, and I want you to climax, I want you to come fully into your body for me. Will you do that for me?'

'Yes, Drew.'

I think my Master and I were fulfilling so many fantasies so fast it took us a while to catch up and learn some profoundly significant lessons that would end up making our erotic adventures even more fulfilling in the future. My nipples were pierced and I wore my Master's slave rings for over a year before he removed them himself because they were causing me more pain than pleasure. After two years, the existential pain I suffered in my soul every time I thought about Swinging with another couple – of enduring the 'full swap' scenario, a term I absolutely hate – reached a climax. The clues hidden in all the fantasies my Master and I had made flesh together finally revealed their lessons, and what I had believed was a rule forever to be an uncomfortable part of my life was lifted from my psyche when my Master said to me, 'Our relationship isn't based on rules, Missa, it's based on promises, and I promise you'll never have to do that again.'

It's important to realize that a Master and slave relationship is not a rigid, static thing based on inflexible objective rules that can never change. I am never forced to obey my Master – I take profound joy in fulfilling our promises to each other. Yet it took me over two years to discern and emotionally digest this vital distinction by truly trusting in his love, and as a consequence I suffered more than I should have. Strangely enough, one of the hardest things for me to grasp has been the fact that Stinger truly does love me and therefore cannot take pleasure from something if I don't take pleasure from it as well.

Excerpt from my Journal:

My Master picked me a bouquet of wildflowers. He knew the names of them all, I only recognized the buttercups, and showed him what he knew not – the yellow light they cast under our chins. Tender moments of peace and happiness after another turbulent Martini Saturday in which I wept and hit him and hated him and loved/desired him more than ever. 'You're not a doormat and I can't handle you that way,' he said. 'You let me take responsibility for when something goes wrong... I'm learning about you...' He promised me I won't ever have to endure being with another undesirable (to me) man again. 'You're not so stupid to think that I can be completely into something if you're not also experiencing pleasure... I care about you, Missa, and you don't have to do that again... What's important is how much I love you.'

I enjoy sharing my wealth; I cannot tolerate being exiled from him. If another man is to use me, my Master cannot be physically separated from me at the same time. That is imperative! I need his focus to be mainly on me and the sacrifice I'm making for his pleasure even if he's also busy fucking another woman. I told him this, and he understands, thank God! I could be perfectly happy for the rest of my life only feeling my Master's cock inside me, but if we are to play with other couples, then it must be done the right way; my Master can't simply be fucking another woman while her partner bangs me. My Master must be touching me or kissing me or be inside me along with the other man for the experience to be even remotely exciting for me.

Thank God for Richard. He is so right, and he has filled my soul with the blessed light of clarity after two years of groping through shadows trying to make myself believe otherwise. 'It's never going to work for you with other men because you love Stinger. There's always going to be the comparison between Stinger and Mr. X and he'll never stand the test, and whether he has a big cock or is virile or not has nothing to do with it because you love Stinger... You're both looking for the same thing, to enjoy yourselves together, and it's good you've both realized sooner than later you can't order that item off the menu' meaning the 'full swap' where Stinger fucks another woman while I fuck another man separately from each other.

I told Richard how when there's another man inside me without my Master also holding or somehow possessing me it's like being exiled from heaven back into this imperfect frustrating world while the other woman gets paradise. Whereas when I'm not exiled to a lesser man (and Richard's right, they will always be lesser one way or the other no matter what) I am part of that paradise as the Goddess who reigns supreme with her beautiful lord and Master sharing her boundless wealth; I double the power of my sensuality, making myself even more special and beautiful by donning the flesh of all womanhood and offering it to my priest of the male force and spirit to use and shape while I partake of his (to me) divine essence. Master and I must more aggressively seek submissive women to play with, one or even two at a time, and better define what we desire to experience with couples. I must ask my Master permission to revise our profile on alt.com...

***

Master did indeed give me permission to edit our profile on alt.com to reflect what we had learned, and this is the revised profile we posted:

Cleopatra meets a sexy angel - one of the angels who fell with Lucifer! Missa says: I'm Stinger's beloved and devoted 24/7 Slave, which means nothing makes me happier than fulfilling his desires, and after over two years in the lifestyle we're pretty clear on what pleases us and what doesn't. We are NOT interested in couples where the man is bi-sexual, we always practice safe sex and we NEVER play in separate rooms; for us it's all about sharing experiences together. We also don't do a 'full swap' in the sense of simply trading partners for a while. One-on-one sex can never be better than it is between us. Swinging is about experiencing things we can't do alone, and we love being with the right couple when me and the other girl get to enjoy the thrill of a double penetration, three-way fun, and the sweet pleasure of playing with each other both by ourselves and while our partners are inside us, etc. etc. We are not into radically distasteful practices such as scat, bestiality, children, blood-letting, piercing, nipple or vaginal torture, punching, humiliation or extreme pain. Yet we ARE truly a 24/7 Master and slave couple seriously into bondage and discipline.

We're looking for lovely submissive women. I love offering my Master another pretty girl to play with, and the girls are never disappointed, believe me! We've been with both vanilla girls and extremely submissive slaves, and we enjoy both in different ways.

We are also looking for couples where both the man and the woman are attractive (no bi-sexual men, please!) We love to meet other Master and slave couples to do things with socially – just talking about our lifestyle is nice – for exhibitionism and voyeurism or intense erotic fun as described above, and if it involves bondage and discipline all the better.

Pics first (including your face, please) then drinks and conversation, and then, who knows, maybe everything we can all possibly desire...

* * *

Master requested I write down some idea of what I would desire for us to do with another couple, and he was so pleased with the results, he indicated we should revise our profile on alt.com again. So of course I did, and was amazed when the website accepted our very graphic descriptions. I posted a slightly edited version of the following with a disclaimer that we did not expect to do all these things every time with a couple, nor was it necessary for them to think of themselves as Master and slave to play with us:

Couple Play Ideas
Living Room Foreplay:

The slaves are commanded by their respective Masters to strip into their slave uniform

The slaves are commanded to sensually fondle each other for their Masters' pleasure

Each slave sucks her own Master's cock

Each slave is fucked by her own Master

Bedroom:

The slaves lie on the bed facing each other, kissing and fondling each other, while their Master's fuck them from behind

One slave sucks her Master's cock while the other Master fucks her from behind. Meanwhile, the slave left out kisses and caresses her Master as well as the slave being doubled AND/OR she lies beneath the slave being doubled and licks her pussy along with her own Master's cock

The slaves assume a 69 position (preferably with the hostess slave on top) and they are each penetrated by the other slave's Master. The bottom slave is penetrated from the front, the top slave from behind, so that each slave can lick her own Master's cock at the same time as the pussy he is fucking; so she can very closely watch her beloved Master's cock sliding in and out of another pussy

One slave licks the other slave's pussy while her own Master fucks her from behind while the slave being orally serviced sucks her own Master's cock. Roles can then be reversed, so that each slave gets a chance to orally serve her Master while being orally served herself.

A variation on the above – One Master goes down on the other Master's slave from behind while she gives her own Master a blow-job and he in turn goes down on the other slave in an oral train

One slave is doubled – preferably her Master's cock in her ass and the other man's cock in her pussy – while she licks the other slave's pussy AND/OR the other slave watches and caresses whomever she desires to caress, including herself, while awaiting her turn to be doubled

One slave enjoys a triple penetration – the other slave in her pussy using a strap-on dildo, her Master in the orifice of his choice and the other Master in the remaining orifice

At the end of the night each Master fucks his own slave, ideally face-to-face.

Each slave experiences face-to-face penetration only with her own beloved Master looking into his eyes, or with the other slave in the case of a strap-on scenario.

As a general rule, each slave only sucks her own Master's cock, unless she is being tripled and her Master wants to be in her ass, in which case she will suck the other Master's cock with a flavored condom. Unprotected oral sex is – as a normal rule, barring any cases of extreme sensual inspiration – limited to pussy licking, although obviously if the other slave does not have a problem giving blow-jobs without a condom, she will be more than free to do so.

***

To Master and me, monogamy means being in love only with each other. Sharing sensual adventures – daring to explore experiences that are theoretically dangerous or even fatal to love and marriage – only deepens the bond forged by our souls and experienced by our flesh in any way we desire. Swinging is not an objective reality – it is always about our connection to each other and the excitement it affords us on every level.

Master said, 'I've come up with supporting roles for other girls. You're the main heroine, the Lady of the Castle vs. a mere serf, the High Priestess vs. a temple whore.' My soul slips on another woman's body like a glove to caress him in a different way than I normally do.

We did not post the following play ideas an alt.com, but they are definitely part of our sensual repertoire:

Master's Single Girl Play Ideas:

We will begin by relaxing with some champagne and appetizers. Then first you, and then she, will present yourselves in slave uniform to me. At that point, I will explain to her that you are my slave goddess and priestess of our temple with fealty only to me, and that she is a new altar girl brought to the temple for training and enlightenment. Thus her role is to be in both of our service. She will determine a safe-word. Then she will be told that our first communion will be a non-challenging sensual exploration.

You and I will then begin our sexual pleasure and she will help. As she is determined willing and able, she will be given more variety in what she is allowed to experience. You will use her to explore and kiss for my pleasure and for sensual effect.

You will both perform fellatio on me simultaneously, and then I will slide into your pussy while she continues to stimulate you.

I will then put you on your knees over her so that she can lick your clitoris while I continue to pump in and out of you.

You will then begin to lick her at the same time with me still inside you. I'll then put on a condom and penetrate her while kissing you.

Finally, to end the first aria, you will sit on my cock and ride to orgasm while she gently plays with your nipples and kisses your neck.

We will then refresh ourselves with drinks, etc.

* * *

Master: Missa

MissaSlave: Master?

Master: I read your email. A very nice possible evening you have suggested, Dear.

We'll keep a little mystery in it but this is a good idea of what could happen. I know that you're going to make us very happy.

Master: I do have a few modifications though… First, as a starting point, I will of course display you to them. Your arms bound behind your back so that your breasts stick out. You will sit as I have taught you with your legs spread. In addition to my own knowing hands caressing you, I will allow both the man and the woman to fondle you and admire your beauty. You will be showing that your lovely body is mine to use and share as pleases me.

Master: Also, assuming that they have transcended that limit, there will also be a point in the evening in which you will suck my cock, place a condom on it and prepare it, and then, with your own hand, guide it into the other girl's ass.

MissaSlave: Yes, Master, thank you, and I believe that second modification was part of #5

Master: It was not clear in #5

MissaSlave: I left the mystery in places, Master

Master: OK

MissaSlave: This outline is like a skeleton to be fleshed out

Master: good pun

Master: Love you

* * *

MissaSlave: Master, may I send that GI who so desperately requested it a picture of my freshly

shaved pussy?

MissaSlave: The picture I sent you last week

Master: yes I suppose so – you know you're going to be posted on every barracks wall in

Iraq soon :-)

MissaSlave: I live to serve ;~)

Master: yes you do – and well

Master: Love you

Master: XOXOXO

MissaSlave: XOXOXO

* * *

The clues to the realization that I need my Master's attention primarily focused on me in order to make having another man inside me tolerably exciting are everywhere evident in my writing. There is never another woman involved when the heroine is being shared with other men by the man she loves, as in this passage from my erotic romance *Pleasures Unknown*:

> She was vaguely aware that the wind had dropped; the two torches were burning with concentrated control as he took her hand and led her back towards dry land. As he rose out of the water's dark mirror before her his naked body glistened beneath the flames, and his long narrow back made her think of a wild cat's spine magically learning to walk on two legs in the blink of an eye. His leanness was all muscle and his dark wet hair clung to his skull sleek as a panther's skin. He turned to face her beneath one of the torches, where they could absorb its warmth. His high cheekbones stood out dramatically, heightening the sensuality of his curving mouth, and the dark trees behind him were almost reverently silent as she slipped her arms around his neck.
>
> The cold water had temporarily dissolved his desire, but she felt it quickly resurrecting against her belly. Yet she didn't want to make it too easy for him, so she pulled away and caressed his chest with her fingernails.
>
> 'Mm...' he said. 'Harder.'
>
> She allowed her nails to rake down his body with a ferocious delight as she glanced up at his face to make sure she wasn't scratching him too deeply, but his gray eyes were a polished silver in the torchlight giving nothing away even as

they let her catch an exciting glimpse of her true nature. Very carefully, she grazed the sides of his stiffening cock with two claw-like hands. It reared up stiffly in response and she let her nails stroke it a little more cruelly relishing the sight of its quivering response. His penis was not so very different from Chris's in appearance. They were both unusually fine examples of the circumcised male organ, the thick, straight shaft crowned by a head shaped like a mushroom cap, and the mere sight of it growing straight out from between the muscular trunks of his thighs was intoxicating to her. Curiously cradling the hard-on she was responsible for, Maia found herself giddily wondering if a great cock was a requirement for membership in this modern Druid cult, which naturally led her to try and picture what Drew's erection would be like… which proved a mistake since he was the man she really wanted inside her.

Eric sensed her hesitation and promptly dealt with it. He turned her around so she was facing the water and put a gentle but determined pressure to bear on both her shoulders.

…She was at once stunned and thrilled by Eric's absolute indifference to her thoughts. He didn't care about any moral battles she might be fighting inside herself anymore than a cat pays attention to the desperate beating of wings from a bird caught in its jaws. He did not actually force her down; she ended up on her hands and knees on the ground because she wanted to. It turned her on that he said not a word and wasn't even bothering to tell her what to do. She knew how he wanted her because it was what her body wanted too. It was intensely relaxing how right and natural it felt to be on all fours in the grass as he positioned himself behind her. She imagined Drew watching her submissiveness to a man's will. For all she knew the high priest was standing in the darkness between the trees observing her obedience to a man's desires, and it was an intensely stimulating thought as Eric filled the entrance to her pussy, then paused to give her time to savor the anticipation of a cock she had never felt inside her before preparing to penetrate her. She moaned to tell him she was ready for the incomparable sensation as in her mind his erection transformed into much more. She felt herself opening up to the unknown as he sank leisurely into her pussy, forcing her dwell on the violation of her moral and romantic being as she let herself be filled with a complete stranger's hard-on. She felt herself opening up to her deepest feelings for Drew, letting go of her resistance to them and blissfully accepting them... the sharp pleasure she suffered amazed her as she allowed her willingness to do whatever Drew wanted her to do completely sink into her soul through another man's cock stabbing her body... a cock the Druid high priest commanded like a scepter with which he ruled her mind and heart as no other man ever had before or ever would again... she fully opened up to the mysteriously beautiful certainty that Drew Landson was her destiny as she let another man penetrate her in his name, as she let another man fuck her so he could know he truly possessed her... she was ecstatically filled with images of the high priest as Eric thrust himself all the way into her pussy, and it was the excitement she experienced in fulfilling Drew's desire that made this other man's vigorous strokes feel so impossibly good...

She was on her hands and knees for a long time as Sir Wolfson enjoyed indulging himself in her slick hole, and the whole time he said not a word. She kept her eyes open as he fucked her long and hard, until there seemed no end in sight to his driving energy and she almost couldn't stand how much she loved it. She was strangely proud of how wet and deep her pussy felt in response to her fantasy that Drew was watching her body being taken on his command. Every beat of her heart and of Eric's cock said I love you, Drew, I love you, I'm doing this for you, I love you! as she sustained the submissive position enabling another man to plunge into her body with nearly vicious force. She loved having a big hard dick inside her. Her innermost flesh felt achingly, meaninglessly empty when a man wasn't packing his rampant cock into her tight cunt and taking her feelings farther than they could ever go alone, and the thought of Drew was deliciously confused in her clitoris with the force pulsing between her thighs, the crackling torches perfectly reflecting the hot sensual rhythm of their coupling bodies...

'Oh yes, yes!' she pleaded softly, clutching the grass and concentrating on the exquisite quivering of her clit as Eric banged her with a casual fierceness that made how gloriously cheap she felt border on the mystical. Somehow managing to hold herself up on one arm trembling with the effort, she reached down to caress herself, and the sensation of his erection swelling to critical mass between her thighs easily pushed her over the edge into her own climax.

Just because something is a fantasy doesn't mean it's a dream without sense or consequences. Master and I have learned through experience that there's a right way and a wrong way for us to play, although that's not to say we haven't thoroughly enjoyed ourselves in the process. I sent my friend and publisher, Richard, the following e-mail:

> *What I meant is that Missa understands the difference between love and sex, but MIP was raised to believe that true love is monogamous, that sex and love should be one and the same, that people who truly love each other should be physically faithful to each other, yadda yadda yadda. And all these moral myths feed the green dragon of jealousy. Missa knows you can't kill the dragon and she's learned to ride it and really enjoy the thrill of having the power to make fantasies real, but sometimes when she's feeling weak she falls off and down into MIP again, which hurts like hell.*

The promises my Master has made me about what I will and will not have to do are the reigns we put on the Dragon of our sexuality so it works for us and we share in what for me is its mystical power. My Master and I are always faithful to each other's feelings, yet getting our personal reigns on the erotic beast hasn't been easy; I've felt psychologically burned a few times along the way, but a couple has to have the strength and courage to fully awaken the dragon if they really want to fulfill their desires together. There are so many relationships and marriages in which the man and the woman ignore the sensual serpent living in their subconscious basement or secretly feed it without each other's knowledge, generally treating sex as a demon forever threatening the pure and safe bond of their love. At least my Master and I are facing and riding the Dragon together, and what I've learned since I wrote Richard that e-mail is that I never fall alone; when my Master and I fall it's always together, and we pick ourselves up, soothing each other's aches, then climb right back into the saddle of our passionate relationship as it spreads hauntingly beautiful conceptual wings into other dimensions.

* * *

One night, after he spent two days attending a meeting full of computer geniuses, my Master seemed totally disinterested in sex, not even asking me to suck his cock even for a few minutes in the evening. We went to bed early, and my overly dramatic fearful self went out of control imagining he had met some hot computer babe. I tormented myself with irrational scenarios of him no longer loving me anymore, etc. etc. I got up to close door to the bedroom to keep in the air conditioning, and in that uncanny way of his my Master – who had been sound asleep – suddenly asked me if I was all right and if something was wrong. He sensed – he knew – I needed to be in his arms. He knew I needed to suck his cock and catch his cum in my mouth as he jacked off, and then to lick him clean of his sweet semen. Then, just like a baby given her bottle, I was able to fall asleep peacefully. It can either be terrifying or mystically inspiring to realize I truly am his slave in that my psyche needs to serve him physically; to absorb the essence of his maleness. I will always be grateful that when I was twenty-two years old I found a book in my mother's library that at the time saved my life by helping me make sense of the brief affair I had with a touring British musician in New York. This incredible book, *The Metaphysics of Sex* by Julius Evola, has since helped me formulate my own beliefs regarding the dangerously powerful energies of love and sex when they are not properly grasped and wielded together.

I've had to train myself not to suffer a jealous tantrum when my Master idly surfs adult websites. I am only one woman with one unique set of features and a figure all my own, but as he has told me countless times, 'It's you I love, Missa' and as his slave-priestess-

Goddess I command, and mysteriously rule over, the ocean of female flesh in which I am just one unique wave. Before he met me, my Master was bored to death deep inside this sea of femininity, and now he says to me, 'Yes, I occasionally like to dip into that ocean again, but only with you, because it's your soul I love. You're the only woman who truly interests me.' At first I admit this sounded like an excuse to me, but I know – and feel – much better now thanks to experiences we have shared with women. It's a lost cause to be jealous of the Internet, like a fish being jealous of the sea, and when we play with another girl I feel beautiful and powerful as a mermaid in the face of just one more slick pussy he's gutting as we enjoy feasting on the powerful depths of our love for each other. And he always wears a rubber when he's diving into another cunt, which means we're monogamous in the sense that the skin of his cock only ever comes into contact with my innermost flesh. Safe sex is at once a physical necessity and a metaphysical fidelity.

By the time I began working on my third erotic romance (this one a completely new work) I felt I had grasped a vital difference between sex and love-making:

'I've thought a lot about sex.'

He laughed softly. 'So have I.'

'No, I'm serious, I–'

'So am I.'

I sighed. 'I really don't think there's such a thing as making love, Gerald.'

He was silent for a moment. 'What do you mean?' he asked.

'I mean there's no such thing as love-making when you're having sex, because sex is sex, and sex is inherently violent, you know; penetration is not a gentle act. I mean, foreplay can sometimes be tender, kissing and caressing, and all that, but sex itself is never tender; if it is, it's impotent and boring.' I paused in an effort to find the right words for how I felt.

'Go on...'

'I believe love-making relates to every other aspect of a couple's life,' I continued, encouraged by his profound attention. 'When a man and a woman truly love each other, everything they do for each other is making love – holding each other at night, cuddling up together to watch a movie, one of them cooking for the other, listening to each other's thoughts and feelings about everything every day for the rest of their lives knowing they'll always be there for each other sharing everything together – all that is love-making, but when they have sex, they're having sex, not making love. Sex is its own mysterious dimension.'

'And you don't think sex is more special between two people who love each other, Ariana?'

'Oh yes, of course I do,' I assured him fervently, looking up into his eyes for an instant before staring off into space again as though reading cosmic cue cards helping me express myself. 'Sex is much more intense between two people who love each other because it's mysteriously charged by their love and deepened by their soulful connection to each other, but it isn't necessarily only an *expression* of their love for each other, although obviously it can be; most of the time it's still purely sex.' I sighed again. 'I really don't know how to express it. I've been reading articles about how pervasive pornography is becoming in our society, not just through XXX films now but also through computers and the internet. So many couples get divorced when the woman finds out her husband is secretly into pornography. They feel betrayed, like they're not good enough for him, and I think they're wrong. I think they don't understand that love and sex can be two totally different things, not just in a man's psyche but in reality. These women believe in the myth of love-making in relation to sex, but making love is mainly about the life you build with someone and how much your souls care especially for each other... I went to a strip club with one of my ex-boyfriends once,' I confessed, 'and afterwards when we went home I felt completely empowered, not in the least degraded. It was as if my body was imbued with the flesh of all those other women... as if my body was all women's bodies and he was passionately worshipping the universal power of my sex through my own personal unique embodiment of it. I think women need to realize that love and sex are two different forces, and that how much a man truly loves them has nothing to do with his need for pure sex. I mean it's ridiculous and damaging to think less of men for obeying a metaphysical principle, isn't it? Women really need to realize they have the power to give the man they love everything he desires and to fulfill their own secret fantasies by not always confusing love-making with sex; by willingly merging their flesh with the flesh of all other women in a sacred, positive interpretation of what feminists consider a degrading objectification of the female body. A man and a woman who truly love each other should think of sex as a safari they enjoy going on together – it's unpredictable, it's wild, it can be dangerous and even violent, but ultimately it's a fun adventure that brings their souls closer together instead of tearing them apart if they're very careful... Am I making any sense at all?'

'Ariana, you make more sense than anyone I've ever met.' He kissed the top of my head. 'But now I think I'd better leave because I'm getting so turned on I won't be able to walk soon.'

* * *

I dreamed it was night and a large building at the summit of a vast hill was burning. I wanted my Master and me to run from the conflagration, yet instead he turned straight towards it, scaled a wall, and vanished. I couldn't believe it. It filled me with despair that he didn't seem to care about the intense fear and worry he was causing me; that his desire for adventure was greater than his concern for my feelings and even for our physical safety. Then suddenly he emerged from behind the wall again carrying a body in his arms and I realized I had been completely wrong about his motivations. He was rescuing unconscious bodies from the burning building, not just foolishly looking for excitement. Then I was walking side-by-side with Daisy, the girl we had met at the Crucible. She was wearing her topless corset and flirting with me and despite myself I was enjoying the feel of her sensuality enhancing my own, knowing it pleased my Master to watch us together. It was a powerfully vivid dream, and when I woke up I knew exactly what it was telling me – that despite how deeply I loved my Master and how much I trusted him, I was still constantly underestimating his motives and motivations. Part of me was still afraid everything he made me do – everything we did together – stemmed from a selfish lust for excitement whether it was dangerous (unhealthy) or not, and that this hunger was greater than his concern for my feelings. I was stunned and ashamed in the dream when I realized how wrong I had been, and in reality I felt the same way knowing I did my Master a terrible injustice by believing he didn't care about my reactions, and by doubting everything we did was related to his love for me and the pleasure we took in doing these things together. I knew perfectly well he had saved me from parts of myself I don't miss. He has saved me by bringing to life parts of me that might have died if I'd never met him. I can't even imagine now what life would be like without him. I would still be burning with the frustration of unrealized dreams and desires.

CHAPTER SIX

Embodying The Goddess

Master and I did indeed have the pleasure of being alone with Daisy in the comfort of our own home. She informed me in an e-mail that her Master was leaving town for a few days, and that he might be persuaded to let her play with us while he was gone. Permission was granted, which seemed only fair since he was headed for a BDSM 'convention' with a submissive male he would be officially dominating throughout the event. The concept was utterly distasteful to me, but Master and I live on our own planet – it would not even cross Stinger's mind to leave me alone for days while he engaged in kinky (perhaps even sexual?) play with another slave. But every relationship is its own unique world, and even though some of the casual laws that applied in John and Daisy's marriage were anathema to the passionate gravity of my nature, I did not hesitate to take advantage of them for my Master's pleasure. I arranged for Daisy to come over for dinner one night, and I felt triumphant as a lioness hauling in a succulent kill the king of my pride and soul could enjoy. Figuratively feasting on her together would strengthen our sensual bond and mysteriously inject fresh blood into our already intense sexual attraction to each other. The saying, 'it can never be like it was in the beginning' is sadly very often true unless you dare work some erotic magic and make a delicious sacrifice on the altar of your loving bed... I knew for a fact that after being intimate with other people my attraction to, and desire for, my Master sharpens almost painfully. The sharpest knife becomes dull with excessive use and needs to be honed on a hard surface to restore it's dangerous edge – God knows the concept of Swinging has been hard for me to embrace and is fraught with dangers, but the results are worth it and much more priceless than the superficial pleasure of the experience. True love between a man and a woman can be likened to the mythical sword Excalibur – its divine edge never truly needs sharpening, but the base metal from which it is made should be properly and passionately cared for, and to that end, every now and then, Master and I play with other people because it hones our love by keeping our sexual appetite for each other painfully sharp. We don't need to Swing to be happy any more than a person needs to exercise to live, but we choose to keep our relationship in the best possible shape; releasing haunting endorphins that turn back the clock and maintain the edge in our sex life so many couples allow to become dull enough that they end up cheating on each other to recapture a sense of excitement. There's no reason it can't always be there with the person you love.

Daisy got lost and was late, which was to be expected, and then a violent thunderstorm blew in that felt like a cosmic reflection of how excited and nervous I was. Master and I went and stood out on the porch to enjoy the caress of the charged atmosphere against our skins, just as a bolt of lightning struck only one street away with a deafening and blinding crash I was afraid might have killed Daisy, for she had just called us from the parking lot. I was looking forward to seeing her again. I hadn't forgotten the unbelievable fact that I had actually craved licking her ass and her pussy. I was pleased by how dramatic the heavens were being on this eventful evening, for it was only the second time I had been able to offer my Master the pleasure of having two women all to himself. The sight of Daisy as she walked up the steps outside was a shock, and unlike the pure spectacle of the lightning, not a pleasant one. She looked cheap in a very short denim skirt and moderate high-heeled sandals, and I don't think it was my imagination she had gained some weight on the Atkins diet. Her thin reddish-blonde hair looked different, and it turns out she had been wearing a hairpiece that night in the attic. I suppose I had idealized her in memory and the reality disappointed me, but no so much that I wasn't pleased to see her, especially since my Master's smile told me he didn't have a problem with the overall quality of the flesh I had politely dragged in for him. I was anticipating the thrill of watching him make the kill. I just wanted to see his big hard cock stabbing all her orifices and subjectively gutting her as he roughly positioned her naked, compliant body however he wanted it.

We all had a pleasant time sitting in the living room drinking champagne and talking, at least that's probably the impression our Shiatsu boy Merlin got as he played with his toy, happy to be in possession of a room full of humans. The truth is I had been hit by another lightning bolt of shock when our guest confessed she was an ex-prostitute. The Daisy who had lived in my imagination since that night in the dungeon attic faded away like a kinky Cinderella all aglow at the BDSM ball turning into her former dirt-streaked self with no real enchantment surrounding her. There had been a delightful innocence to Linn, the one other single girl Master and I had played with in private so far, and Daisy's slightly jaded, once professional aura was a serious turn-off for me. I wondered how Stinger felt about it even as in many ways I enjoyed our conversation. Daisy is a very nice, very intelligent woman, and if she didn't fit my bill for an ideal fantasy playmate, she was nevertheless extremely likeable and easy to get along with.

When it came time for me to go to the kitchen to melt cheese for the fondue, Master and Daisy stood on the other side of the island watching me. By this time he had requested (commanded) she remove her shirt, and beneath it she was wearing a chain-mail brazier around her breasts that linked with the heavy silver collar around her neck. In contrast I was modestly clad in a clinging peach-colored dress accented by a hip-belt of thin old bronze coins that made a subtle tinkling noise as I moved around the kitchen. It was impossible for me to be jealous of Daisy; she and Master never seemed to take their eyes off me as I slavishly stirred the cheese, and they occasionally interrupted the conversation to comment on my desirable features, which combined with how much champagne I had drunk was taking the edge off my nerves.

We had a deliciously sinful dinner of Cheese Fondue with hunks of toasted French bread and oven-broiled shrimp accompanied by a bottle of red wine. By the time we stood up and carried our glasses into the bedroom, I was feeling totally relaxed, and suddenly possessed by a very different kind of hunger. I set my glass down and said, 'Would you like to share some dessert with me, Daisy, and help me go down on my Master?' or something to that effect. She replied by promptly sinking to her knees and impatiently helping me pull down my Master's pants and underwear. Then my face was buried between the cheeks of his ass as I rimmed him passionately, how fulfilled I was by food and drink somehow intensifying how starved I was for the feel and taste of his flesh. I had positioned the three of us next to a mirror so he could watch me licking his anus while Daisy sucked his cock, and *sucking* him she was, making loud slurping sounds as her head bobbed swiftly up and down his erection, visible to me in the mirror as I surfaced from the deliciously thick atmosphere of my Master's buttocks. I saw his hands were on her head, but then he reached behind him with one and urged my face back into his crack.

'Oh yes…' he said as I thrust the tip of my tongue inside him, struggling to penetrate him and feel the inside of him, relishing the sense of my efforts making his cock even harder and more sensitive to the oral attentions of my second mouth, which I was happy to hear working very hard to please him. That is how Master perceives another woman's orifices, as 'Missa's other pussy' or 'Missa's other mouth.' Going down on him with Daisy I experienced nothing but the sheer delight of having my sensual power over him effortlessly doubled.

'Change places,' he commanded, and I was happy my Master wanted to feel my mouth around his cock while Daisy performed the less glamorous task of tonguing his ass. (He later told me she did not do nearly as good a job as I did, which further pleased me in retrospect.)

Not long afterwards, I found myself sitting on the edge of my bed while Daisy knelt before me licking my pussy, but the only thing that excited me about it was the sight of Master (somehow we were all naked by now) reaching for a condom. I encouraged him with a wordless gesture and a happy conspirator's smile to quickly slip it on and penetrate her from behind while she was busy going down on me. It aroused me to watch him kneeling behind her, and then to reach down so I could help guide his erection into her hole, although all I really got to do was touch it briefly as he thrust hard into Daisy's pussy. She reacted by throwing her head back and gasping from the glorious shock, and very soon she was incapable of doing anything except crying out as Stinger banged her. I felt myself grinning triumphantly as I slipped off the bed so Master could fling her up across it and stand up as he fucked her from behind, his eyes on me and his smile reflecting mine the whole time. He gripped her hips and beat his body against hers while I watched the spectacle reclining across his waterbed, delighted by how devastated Daisy obviously was by his unrelentingly swift penetrations. She was making such a racket, in fact, that I became concerned for her. Sitting up, I gently caressed the hair away from her perspiring face.

'Are you all right?' I murmured. 'Do you like that, sweetheart?' To which she replied with a fervent nod, her cries escalating in urgency as Master began driving into her with even greater force when I went and stood beside him, caressing him and seeking to merge my flesh with his as I delighted in watching him enjoy my offering, and in listening to her helpless response to his thrusts. This beautiful virile man was mine every day and every night for the rest of my life, and I felt infinitely sorry for her knowing she could only feel him inside her this once, or maybe a few more times if he was generous. I felt like a priestess handing out a few gold coins of my boundless wealth at the temple where I worshipped the Goddess latent within me, my sensuality hauntingly doubled and empowered by another woman's body; a body I had brought to the altar of the bed I shared with my Master and soul mate, making the ultimate sacrifice in the face of jealousy and achieving the divine end of an even greater feeling of love and intimacy between us.

I had begun to worry what the neighbor's might think – Daisy sounded as though she was being exquisitely stabbed to death – when Master finally pulled out of her and reached for a tube of lubricant. He commanded me to lick her pussy while he prepared her anus for his cock, and I willingly complied, curious to see how I felt about licking her sex that night. It was not as enjoyable to me as the last time for a number of reasons, not the least of which was the flavor of her less than ideal past. But it was fun looking up from her crotch to watch Master fingering her impossibly small sphincter, casually slipping the end of his lubricated finger into her tight little hole. I was thrilled by the prospect of watching him fuck another woman in the ass for the first time, yet it was not to be, for Daisy squirmed away from him at the last teasing minute.

'That's too fast for me,' she protested, and I sighed as another anal mermaid wriggled away leaving me hungry for that particular fantasy. Nevertheless, there were plenty of others left to make flesh. I asked Daisy to lie on her back on my bed, taller than my Master's waterbed, with her head hanging off it so he could kneel on his mattress and slip his erection straight down her throat, ideally offered up in this position for his slow, careful strokes. I watched his face as he watched mine, and I was at once pleased and disappointed he looked a touch bored behind his gratified smile. He later told me it would have been much more exciting for him with a girl who had to make some effort to orally accommodate his dimensions. 'It felt good but it wasn't great,' he said. 'I mean, you could stick a baseball bat down her throat; there was no friction' and I had to agree. The knowledge that we were playing with a woman who had once been a prostitute took much of the thrilling edge off the sex for me; the rare experience was somewhat tarnished, but we made the best of it. Master had pulled off the condom so she could deep throat him, but he quickly grew bored with this activity and pulled Daisy down onto the waterbed with us. He urged me onto my hands and knees so he could fuck me from behind, and she slipped beneath us to eagerly tongue both my vulva and his balls as his hard cock thrust in and out of my pussy for a wonderful stretch of time.

Master had bought me a crotchless strap-on that finally lost its virginity that night as Daisy lay on her back on the waterbed and I knelt between her legs while Master positioned himself behind me, penetrating me with his flesh-and-blood erection as I more tentatively inserted the bright pink rubber cock into Daisy's accommo-dating slot. I imagine that if the body of the woman beneath me had really turned me on, the act of thrusting into it with a lifeless dildo might have excited me enough mentally to make up for the lack of physical sensation. Nevertheless, I've decided I don't much enjoy wielding a senseless plastic instrument. I found it hard to control the movement of my hips because I had no idea what the rubber penis was up to buried deep in Daisy's cunt. It was inter-esting falling into rhythm with my Master plunging in and out of me as I dove in and out of another woman's sex at the same time, but the pleasure was not worth the effort, in my opinion. It became a bit more fun when she turned over on her side and I fucked her from behind while watching her suck my Master's cock. For a few moments I found my rhythm and did the best I could to please her observing the pink dildo sliding in and out of her. If her pussy had been sweeter and tighter – if Master and I had sensed she was genuinely overwhelmed with pleasure by our combined attentions instead of just performing, as we couldn't help suspect at least a part of her was doing – the subjective excitement might have compensated for the lack of sensual sensation on my part, but that night it didn't.

After dubious strap-on fun, Daisy got up to use the bathroom, perching on the toilet in Master's bathroom facing the bed on which we lay comfortably in each other's arms, enjoying an inti-mate respite from all the three-way fun we were trying to cram into one night. I loved it when he said, 'I have to fuck you again, Missa' and pushed me onto my back so he could plunge his undying hard-on between my thighs. Then Daisy joined us again and I rolled over onto my side so he could keep penetrating me from behind while she kissed and fondled my breasts lying in front of me. When

Master remarked that he had been neglecting Daisy and pulled out of me to reach for a condom, I went completely cold inside as the dual fangs of jealousy and rage sank into me with paralyzing intensity. My body went rigid and I just lay there, completely unresponsive either verbally or physically, a mute rage blazing in my eyes. Master later told me he was joking, for obviously he had paid ample attention to Daisy, but whether he was or not, I was still profoundly distressed by my response and how completely unable I was to control it despite the fun we had all obviously been having.

'Kneel in front of us, Missa,' my Master commanded as he and Daisy sat on the edge of the taller mattress, leaving me alone on the waterbed smoldering with feelings I couldn't quite get a mental grip on. 'Isn't she beautiful?' he asked our guest, smiling lovingly down at me.

'Yes, she is,' Daisy replied dutifully but, it seemed, sincerely.

'I'm madly in love with her.'

'I can tell. And I'm sure she's madly in love with you… I remember the night I first saw you two at the *Crucible*. Missa was wearing that sexy Catholic school girl skirt and those incredible heels, and you looked so hot with your long hair and black leather pants… I thought *I have to meet them!*' She looked from my face to Stinger's, and back again. 'You're a very intense couple…'

I suffered the distinct impression we were a bit too intense for her taste. I think she would have preferred a couple less focused on each other and more into just having sex for the fun of it – for the mere physical pleasure of it – which was not where we were coming from at all.

'I want you to tie Missa's wrists behind her back,' Master instructed, handing her a black-leather shackle, and she did as she was told like a good slave while I trembled inside in the feverish grip of jealousy mixed with love and excitement. 'Very good,' he said. 'Now I want you to kneel in front of me and suck my cock while Missa watches.'

It was a good idea to render me powerless, which sharpened the perverse pleasure I took in watching another woman orally pleasuring my beautiful Master, the only problem was I couldn't see anything since I was kneeling directly behind Daisy; all I could see was her bobbing head and my Master's smiling face above it. I moved angrily, making the almost impossible effort to slide across the yielding mattress without using my hands in order to try and get a better view.

'Missa, did I give you permission to move?'

'No, Master, but I can't see anything from there!' I snapped, furious with him for not realizing it, and apparently he considered my attitude unacceptable, because the next thing I knew I was sprawled face-down across my bed, my high-heeled feet planted on the floor while Master prepared to give me an enema as punishment.

'Mm, look at this view,' he commented, caressing my ass.

'Very nice,' Daisy agreed, but to my ears she did not sound entirely pleased by all the attention I was getting.

I moaned, humiliated yet also perversely pleased to be the center of attention as water filled my rectum, and despite the growing discomfort if felt infinitely better than the cold flood of jealousy I'd suffered earlier. Master had helped me up and was escorting me to the bathroom when Daisy abruptly announced she had to get going. I quickly relieved myself, and by the time I emerged she was dressed and ready to go. She explained she had to get up early the next morning to drive to New York, and whether it was true or not, her departure was unnaturally abrupt. I was upset and angry about it, yet after an initial 'Oh, you don't really have to go yet, do you?' my Master seemed perfectly content to conclude the social part of our evening. We slipped on some clothes, put Merlin on a leash, and walked her down to her car. Then she was gone and Master was soothing my furious disappointment that she had thwarted my plans to please him even more that night.

Back upstairs we both got naked again, and he fucked me passionately, coming violently inside me at last. Afterwards, we sat cozily together on the loveseat in the living room talking, talking, and talking... I always need to talk a lot after Swinging.

'Playing with a single girl is only one of the many fun things we do together, Missa, it's not the *most* fun thing; that's your perspective. And when will you stop being afraid that just because we do something every now and then means we'll have to do it all the time? That's not the case and you know it. When was the last time we played with a girl?'

'Almost a year ago,' I admitted.

'See?' He held me tenderly but firmly against him, my head resting on his chest.

'But I should have been able to control my jealousy tonight,' I murmured miserably.

He laughed softly. 'Missa, do you realize how far you've come? I'm so proud of you and so happy with you. Do you realize how many women wouldn't even think of doing what you do for me?' He squeezed my shoulders. 'You were wonderful tonight and you pleased me very, very much, and I love you.'

'But we *could* have had a lot more fun if she hadn't just left like that,' I snapped.

'Maybe, maybe not, the point is we had a lot of fun together, and you shouldn't spoil that by feeling you've done something wrong and I'm not pleased with you or perfectly satisfied with the evening, because I am. What doesn't please me is you always being afraid of not having pleased me enough, or afraid you'll have to do this all the time in order to truly please me. I want you to be happy with yourself, Missa, and realize how proud of you I am and how much I love you. I want you to enjoy each experience for what it is without worrying about everything so much.'

'Yes, Master...' I was silent for a while, remembering. 'I keep thinking of you banging her,' I confessed. 'I keep seeing you fucking her from behind...'

'Is that a bad thing?' he asked quietly.

'No...' The truth was that it turned me on in an irresistibly agonizing way. 'Do you fuck me that hard?' I asked vulnerably, a stupid part of me afraid my pussy had lost its novelty and Daisy had gotten what I was no longer able to enjoy.

'Yes, I do, Missa, but I love you and I like to savor every inch and moment with you. With Daisy I was banging her and that's all it was.'

* * *

Excerpts from my Journal:

I feel my beauty when I am with my Master and another woman; I feel the beauty of my soul and how much more beautiful (special and powerful) I am to him than just another body.

***

'A slave knows that with her Master nowhere is she safe and yet nowhere is she safer.'
N.T. Morley

***

The way Stinger and I can talk and talk and there is never a dull moment between us when we're enjoying the fruits of the earth and each other.

***

I told Master he had a cat-like way of being, the high metabolic rate of his sharp intelligence making him need as much sleep as a feline to mend the destruction caused by free radicals. I love how he can be as relaxed as a tiger and totally in control at the same time. '(He) seemed oddly aware of his surroundings. Maybe that's a necessary quality in a top. How can you surrender all thought, all judgment, if you aren't sure that someone is making trustworthy decisions for you?' *Mary Mohanraj*

***

I'll never forget the night my Master told me he could easily see how the soul survives the death of the body. Details don't matter, what matters is that if he can easily believe it's possible then it truly is and it's not just wishful thinking on my part. The only thing that really makes me happy is being with Stinger. If love is not eternal then the universe is meaningless. I don't believe in biological life as a justifiable end in itself.

***

My goal is never to rush through anything I do but to enjoy it thoroughly, sensually and completely, because every second of my life is irreplaceable. My New Year's resolution – Beauty & Submission free of tedious fears and insecurities.

* * *

Master and I like to go out for a late breakfast on Saturday and Sunday mornings, that is, of course, after I've 'woken him up' by going down on him, and usually after I've enjoyed two or three orgasms drowning the week's stresses in a vortex of pleasure from which I emerge profoundly relaxed, and starving. I find the lack of sexual education I received from my parents and society utterly appalling. It took a chance viewing of a porno film – in which I saw a woman caressing her clitoris while she was being very properly fucked – to teach me that a real man wouldn't think I was criticizing his virility if, to a certain extent, I took matters into my own hands. For years I thought something was wrong with me because I couldn't come by way of penetration alone. Granted, I've seen women who come like bunnies breed, but I know I'm not alone in my need for more complex stimulation, mental, emotional and physical. One of my favorite things (of many) is riding my Master's cock in public surrounded by mirrors and at least one or two other attractive naked women sitting on top of their partners. I love watching their breasts bobbing up and down just like mine in the mirrors as they work their pussies up and down the hard-ons impaling us. The intense sensuality stoked between Master and me seems reflected and multiplied and made even more devastatingly powerful as their pleasure flows around and merges with ours, rushing like an ancient and timeless river between my thighs as I climax, torn between the sight of my Master's unique smile and all my 'other' bodies. On weekend mornings, Master usually asks me if I want to ride his cock, and when I do, I touch myself, glancing at my desirable body in the mirror as he caresses my breasts and plays with my nipples like two taut, sensitive knobs mysteriously linked to my sex and the orgasmic charge slowly building up between my legs. I close my eyes and imagine how my body would look to others watching me impaled on his erection and willingly stabbing myself with it. And all these stimulations – of my breast, my clitoris and my imagination – magically come together every time I look down at my Master and feel him beneath me and inside me. When I finally come, it's devastating. Obviously, I have no qualms about the voyeur and exhibitionist aspects of Swinging.

One lazy Saturday morning at breakfast, I was thinking of Daisy. 'The difference between a total slut and a good girl,' I mused out loud, 'is that the good girl will only be a total slut for the man she loves, the other girl will be a total slut for just any man.'

'That's true,' Master replied, 'in concept.'

'What do you mean?' I asked warily.

'What if the man she loves wants her to be a total slut with another man?'

'That's different,' I said at once, 'because she's still doing it for him, not to please the other man.'

He smiled. 'Exactly.'

I refrained from adding, 'As long as you're inside me, too, or somehow physically connected with me and not just off fucking some other woman.' The sentence burned through my brain like a comet as I firmly reminded myself to trust him and let harmlessly pass by. We had already discussed the issue and our profile on alt.com had been revised accordingly. He knew, understood, and respected how I felt; therefore, I did not need to worry about another severely distressing scenario ever cropping up in our Swinging life again. 'You know, I feel as though I was raised to be either a nun, a whore or a mother,' I remarked instead. 'Only your love enables me to assume the powers of an ancient priestess, Stinger.'

'You're my Goddess.'

'Yes… but the goddess has another side to her, too, you know. She's not just sensuous beauty and loving compassion, she has a dark, cruel side to her…' I couldn't stop myself; I had to tell him exactly how I felt, and he would agree I was being a good slave in doing so. 'The times we've done the full swap thing and there was another man just thrashing away inside me, the Goddess in me was furiously insulted… you've no idea how angry it can make me, the terrible rage I can feel, watching you and your big beautiful cock thrusting into another lucky woman while I suffer through what for me is a frustrating hell. With another girl it's different, I'm sharing the wealth and I'm connected to you, always with you, a part of you, with another man it's not like that, I'm always settling for less, trading my god for a mere mortal who can never compare… without you inside me at the same time I feel like I'm deliberately throwing away my soul. It's awful! I can't believe it took me so long to realize that what I dread so much about Swinging with another couple is the missionary position, being face-to-face with some strange man looming over me as if he's my whole life, my whole universe… I can't stand it, Master! I'll sit on another man, and he can fuck me from behind, and I'll even suck his cock with a flavored condom, but I can't just lie beneath him in miserable exile from my soul while you become some other woman's universe.'

'Missa, I told you, you'll never have to do that again, I promise. I love you.'

'I can't wait until we have a real play room and we can move away from vanilla swinging, Master. I really need to be in some kind of bondage, helpless to resist, whenever there's another man involved because what turns me on is being absolutely submissive to your desires. It doesn't excite me at all to pretend I want to fuck other men just for sexual pleasure, because I don't.' I sniffed, feeling I had ruined the pleasantly languid mood of our Saturday morning. 'I'm sorry I'm so difficult, Master.'

'You're the love of my life, Missa; dealing with you is always a pleasure.'

CHAPTER SEVEN

Head Kisses

Another excerpt from the illuminated manuscript of my own personal Dark Ages...

It was close to midnight and freezing when Alley-Cat and I arrived in Chicago, two foxes adventurously leaving our safe and warm Miami dens behind. Our cab slowed down in front of houses that looked haunted, bare trees with torturously twisted limbs against shutters sealed as tightly as the eyes of corpses. We were enthralled, hardly believing it when the cab stopped before one of these haunted houses. Carrying our black luggage, we made our way down an alley running alongside what appeared to be a burned out church. The cold wind blew through the broken ribs of its beams, the warm breath of incense long ago exhaled into the indifferent darkness, no candles burning a conscious soul in the empty windows...

On our second night in the apartment we christened The Tree House, Alley-cat and I each swallowed a blue star (acid) and had a torch burning ceremony on the kitchen table, a rough slab of wood we'd propped up. Soon we had two fires burning in small, round ashtrays. The flames were enthrallingly beautiful, luminous and passionately warm, and with the blue stars inside us, we felt our bodies vibrating at their same frequency. We named each flame and, laughing, cut up a brown paper bag into little square pieces pretending it was whole wheat bread so we could feed our flames wax sand-wiches. We felt them growing older... now they were adoles-cents, greedily consuming their food... now they were matur-ing slowly; there was an increasing nobility and power in the way the flames licked higher and higher. At the same exact moment, Alley-cat and I felt they had reached their 21st birth-day.

I spotted a box of religious candles on the kitchen shelf. 'Give me those,' I commanded, and handled the smooth white bodies with a rapt sensual pleasure. 'We're going to give them each a virgin for their coming of age.'

'All right!' Alley-cat was wide-eyed with happiness.

The game went on and on, until we realized the flames were reversing their direction, sinking down into the black mound of ashes. We watched quietly, until there was only a warm red glow left. Staring into the black cliffs of ash, the actual size of the ashtray meant nothing – we were looking at black burial mountains into which the flames were receding with funereal slowness. I could make out ledges and the tiny entrances to caves in the black cliffs. Finally, in a perfectly silent explosion, my flame was gone. I mourned it for a few moments, but it had seemed to recede so eagerly, snake-like, into the black mountain of ash that I felt it was still alive in it somewhere, waiting to be reborn as another flame. We then left the smoke-filled room and went out for a walk in the cold darkness... for us, nothing was a coincidence. We used the term Magic Pattern...

After all these years, I still believe in the Magic Pattern (how could I not when it somehow led me to my Master and soul mate) and I recapture that sense of wonder in the sensual mystery of existence every time I help wake Master up in the morning by sucking his cock, and when I feel his erection pulsing and thrusting in my pussy. The more I open up and let him take his pleasure as forcefully as he wants to the better it feels for me.

God knows I've lived through very dark moments in my life. For years my favorite band was *Joy Division*. But it was precisely because I felt and believed in my creative soul, and the natural world as its mysterious mirror, that I was depressed by its plight in the modern world. I wrapped myself up in an isolating cocoon of poetry and philosophy in an effort to grow beyond my helpless unhappiness, and it was years before my thoughts and feelings were able to soar as one on the wings of love and art. This is a metaphor, but it is also the reality of my life as I choose to live it despite all the ignorant atrocities being committed against human beings by other human beings every day everywhere. In *Recipe For Romance* I express just how I feel about my relationship with Stinger, which bloomed in Miami under very similar circumstances:

On the television screen a bomb was going off on some nameless street in a part of the world I couldn't fathom living in. Then a woman dressed in black robes from head-to-toe was angrily holding up a photograph. Apparently, her husband had died in the blast. The volume was turned down so low I could barely hear her, but unfortunately I did. 'Now I'm one of those women who wants to be a suicide bomber!' she declared even while cradling a baby in one arm.

There was a quiet knock on the front door.

'That's him,' my mom said grimly, and I knew her tone related to the story on the news not to the man standing outside our house on the same planet yet in a totally different world.

I quickly rose to open the door, and when I saw Gerald standing on the threshold, I felt light-years removed from the pain and suffering the media constantly exposes us to. I was obeying completely different laws when I stepped towards him, and his arms came around me like the horizons of another dimension. That night he was wearing a black suit, and the way it contrasted with my white bodice for a magical instant elevated my senses to an arousing metaphysical point inside me free of all doubts and worries. His arms were a pure, dark force cradling me against his chest, and the sound of his heart beating was the pulse of time itself as I rested in the infinitely promising space of his arms.

* * *

It was wonderful sharing my bed with Gerald, especially falling asleep in his arms with my head resting against his chest, but that's not to say it wasn't also a bit of a trial. I sleep deeply and dream constantly (so much so that until I met my beautiful sculptor waking up was often a disappointment in light of all my exciting nocturnal adventures) and I toss and turn a lot at night. With this very special man lying in my bed, I didn't sleep as well as I normally do because I had to make an effort not to move around too much and disturb him. As a result I lay awake for long stretches at a time debating how long to wait before shifting positions again, judging by his breathing how deeply asleep he was and if my motion would disturb him or not. I also lay awake thinking about the fact that commonly accepted rules of long-term relationships often contribute to the difficulty many people seem to have in staying together. I decided when the time was right I would take the subject up with Gerald about sleeping in separate beds when we moved in together. I reasoned that just because you love someone profoundly and want to spend the rest of your life with them doesn't mean you need to be condemned to sleeping next to them every night worrying about disturbing them, and as a consequence not getting enough rest yourself, which in turn puts unnecessary pressure on you and robs you of your full energy, therefore probably making you grouchy… the domino effect of the seemingly innocent rule couples should sleep in the same bed struck me as rather ghastly as I lay there pondering all the potential negative repercussions. I also decided if our finances permitted it would be a good idea to have separate bathrooms as well, a very good idea. I concluded true love and logical thinking should not cancel each other out like matter and anti-matter, but rather they should work together to create a whole other, much better universe than traditionally conceived possible.

At one point during that long but wonderfully fulfilling and constructive night, I finally fell asleep for good. I awoke an indeterminate amount of time later to the sweet singing of birds in the trees outside my windows, although if the truth be told it sounded more like a cacophony as incessantly chirped messages urgently communicating the whereabouts of succulent worms and flowers annoyingly disturbed my restful slumber. The noise made by the poetically idealized feathery army woke me up, and kept me up even though my room was still dark thanks to the abundant foliage surrounding it, which proved a double-edged sword since it was also incredibly noisy with life. I turned over onto my side and lay there contentedly for a while gazing at Gerald's sleeping profile, or at least what I could see of it. He had one of my pillows draped over his eyes and the top of his head, and he would obviously have buried himself beneath it if he hadn't also needed to keep breathing. He lay on his back with the cotton jersey sheet pulled all he way up to his chin, his hands clutching it like a little boy determined not to have it snatched away by some nameless nocturnal enemy. I smiled imagining all the myriad of little endearing things I would discover about him over time. His nose and mouth were beautifully shaped, truly statuesque, as was the rest of his firm but also deliciously tender physique. It was as if the depth of his being and compassion were embodied in his skin, which was softer than the skin of any man I had ever been with and yet not at all delicate or effeminate. *God is keeping his mortal clay nice and moist and supple,* I thought, and *He made this man especially for me, just as all my unique thoughts and feelings and sensations were mysteriously made especially for him...*

The high-pitched chirping of happy birds continued wreaking sentimental havoc with my mental synapses for about thirty minutes before I finally decided to get up and shower while my handsome soul mate slept for however long he felt like it.

In the bathroom, I turned on the hot water thinking about another relationship myth in need of dispelling – that lovers always shower together and enjoy having sex while they do so. In my opinion sex in the tub can definitely be fun, but it is also, I feel, highly overrated. In my book it ranks right down there with trite games such as covering your lover with whipped cream, then licking it off. It seems to me you need to love whipped cream much more than the person underneath

it since the sugary taste of chemicals overrides the more subtle flavor of bare flesh.

I was intensely happy (if a touch cranky and unsympathet-
ic in my thinking) on that beautiful sunny morning in May in my
air conditioned bathroom in already brutally hot south Florida.

When I returned to my bedroom, temptingly wrapped in an
innocent white towel, I was somewhat disappointed to find
Gerald still buried beneath a pillow and showing no signs of
life whatsoever. I wandered idly over to my dresser, where a
morbid curiosity made me pick up my cell phone and carry it
out into the living room. The shrill beep that resounded
through the silent house when I switched it on told me I had a
voicemail message, and I dreaded it. I had not forgotten Eric's
promise to call me again to see if I had changed my mind
about seeing him, and sure enough, I recognized his number
on the Received Calls display. It was a relief to discover he
had not actually left a message, which I hoped meant he had
given up on me. The fact that I was not answering my phone
should tell him I had not changed my mind and was beyond
the possibility of him talking me into doing so.

Switching off my electronic butler again, I returned to the
bedroom, and this time was delighted to see Gerald was
awake, if just barely; at least the pillow was no longer over his
eyes.

'What time is it?' he asked so quietly I barely heard him.

'Nine o'clock,' I replied cheerfully, perching on the edge of
the bed and smiling down at him.

'Why are you wearing that towel?' he demanded after a
moment; it had taken his sleepy brain cells that long to regis-
ter the affront.

I promptly stood up and discarded the damp terrycloth.

He flung the sheet off his naked body. 'Come here.'

I snuggled happily next to him, but apparently he didn't just want me to lie beside him because he placed one of his hands gently on my head, and urged my face down towards his cock. 'Wake me up,' he commanded, and I gladly took his already semi-stiff penis between my lips. My mouth was slightly dry, so I concentrated on sucking his head for a minute, holding firmly onto his shaft to lubricate it with my saliva with the first sweet taste of his semen as he responded to my ministrations. It pleased me how quickly I was able to make him hard, and occasionally I opened my eyes as I sucked him to admire the beautiful cock in my mouth. The soft sounds of pleasure he emitted every now and then assured me I was doing a good job of pleasing him as well as myself. I kept up a steady rhythm of stroking him with my fist and swallowing him whole, alternating between caressing his head with the inside of my cheek and the more stimulating entrance to my throat.

When he finally sat up and urged me onto my hands and knees, I was more than ready for his hard thrust from behind. With my cheek pressed against the bed, I arched my back and offered him full, unrestrained access to my sex; assuming a position in which he could plunge all the way into my slick pussy. He fucked me fast and deep, until all I had to do was reach down and touch my clitoris to start coming. He didn't say a word, utterly focused on his penetrations as I consciously used my vaginal muscles to squeeze his cock, thrilling myself with my power to grip and caress his erection with my deepest self. I milked his deliciously rigid penis from the base to the head with a ripple-like motion of my innermost flesh I could feel was irresistible to him. The sensation of him beginning to climax combined with the urgent motion of my fingertips stimulated my clitoris so much I was able to orgasm with him, an incomparable experience beyond description.

That was such a lovely weekend I can hardly remember anything about it except how happy I was; how utterly relaxed and content with the present as well as excited about the future.

Before I met my Master, and was living in my little 'Doll's House' in Miami, I had come to enjoy my own company, and much preferred being with myself and Merlin than to being with the wrong man, which I had learned was infinitely worse than being alone. When I was by myself I could at least *be* entirely myself instead of struggling to fit into the often mysteriously cramped space of someone else's particular predilections and perceptions. The man I kept dreaming of would appreciate all of me, in every sense, I was sure of this; he would treasure every idiosyncrasy of my personality along with every unique curve of my flesh and I would never have to pretend with him about anything. In all my previous relationships with men, I invariably compromised; restructuring my thoughts and feelings in little ways that did not seem significant in themselves, but after the inevitable breakup, when I added them all up, the result was always the same – a relationship and a routine at odds with my deepest being, which continued stubbornly expressing itself through dreams of true love.

Now that I am fortunate enough to live with my beloved Master, I strive to make our life together as sensually enjoyable as possible, and at one point I realized there was something missing in the way I greeted him every evening when he came home. Unless it's that time of the month, or he has given me permission not to, I always greet him naked except for one of my collars and a pair of high-heels. Yet how happy I was to see him, how much I'd missed him and mysteriously pined away without his company despite how productive I had been throughout the day... the depth of my devotion to him was not being adequately expressed merely by walking up to him and slipping my arms around his neck and kissing him. Mentally and spiritually I am on equal footing with him, but emotionally I feel much more like a cat longing to purr around his ankles and curl up in the mingled warmth, safety and excitement of his lap. I told my Master how I felt, and how I desired to greet him from now on, and he was very pleased by my sentiments and the way I wished to express them in the future. When my Master comes home from work, I still greet him naked except for one of my collars and high-heels, only now I crawl towards him on all fours, and kneel at his feet as I help him remove his clothing, beginning with his watch, shoes and socks, followed by his pants and underwear and finally his shirt. Once he's naked – relieved of the day's clinging burdens by my loving hands – I reverently kiss his feet thinking of Mary Magdalene after she washed those of Jesus, because I can never let myself forget how blessed I am to have found the love Stinger and I share in this world. Then I sit up and kiss the head of his cock, which gives me more pleasure than I had ever dreamed possible, and afterwards I kiss the firm, sensitive hands capable of holding all my best and deepest feelings within them. Only then do I rise to stand face-to-face with him and slip my arms around his neck as our lips meet in a kiss and he presses me hard against him.

Master forged a silver collar for me, taking much time and effort to find just the right tiny heart-shaped lock for it to which only he has the key. After a little over a year together, he replaced my black leather training collar with this, my official collar, which only he has the power to remove. When I wear it against my skin, I can always feel it was made by his hands especially for me, and knowing I cannot remove it of my own free will symbolically merges my life indelibly with his. Stinger and I love each other, but this is not a static reality; every day our love is evolving and deepening. And how conscious we are of how intensely in love we are is mysteriously very important. Being a truly loving couple is a physical and emotional joy as well as a haunting form of spiritual discipline – two souls using the rock of their relationship to hone their sense and grasp of boundless beauty and meaning in everything. As a slave, I have long since outgrown the resentful feminist approach to housework believing I should share all the chores with my mate. Stinger and I contribute equally but differently to our relationship, and if superficially it resembles a marriage from the nineteen-fifties, in spirit it is anything but. Cooking and interior decorating come easily to my sensual and artistic temperament, and I've learned to take a Zen-like pleasure in cleaning by reminding myself that every little aspect of life and every small act I perform is a gift of unfathomable dimensions, being alive the most exciting mystery imaginable.

Colin Wilson writes, 'Man often feels this same ecstasy of affirmation as he confronts the universe: sheer delight in its complexity, and the desire to plunge into it with a splash. But… he gets tired; the excitement fades. And this failure is purely a lack of self-discipline. An adult can increase his mental stamina by deliberate training… No animal possesses that capacity for reaching out ecstatically to grasp the universe. Their instincts are sharper than ours, and they are closer to nature. But they can never know that supreme delight of the imagination taking fire and becoming drunk with its own visions. *That* is what human evolution is about... His (man's) sense of beauty is the direct outcome of his evolutionary urge. It is related to the power of grasping and mastering complexity... 'occultism' is not an attempt to draw aside the veil of the unknown, but simply the veil of banality... Aldous Huxley once made the suggestion that if the human mind has a 'basement' – the Freudian world of instincts and repressions – why should it also not have an attic: a 'superconscious' to balance the 'subconscious'? The powers of the 'superconscious' are within reach of the human will, provided it is fresh and alive... general passivity or defeat-proneness or depression will blunt them... All disciplines aimed at increased use of these powers depend upon a high level of optimism and will-drive.'[#4]

* * *

The night before Hurricane Isabel hit the northeastern U.S., wind was rattling all the window panes like Cathy's spirit confusing my handsome long-haired Master with her beloved Heathcliff.

'Missa,' he said, 'put on some clothes. We're going for a walk on the forest trail.'

'What?' I asked in disbelief. 'There's a hurricane coming!' Naturally, a few minutes later I was outside walking in the crook of my Master's arm feeling invigorated by the elemental passions surrounding us, and wondering why I always believed I was afraid of everything when the truth is I'm in *love* with everything. Or so I felt until we stepped beneath the thrashing canopy of trees and left the streetlights behind. I couldn't see a thing; I felt completely blind.

'Stinger, it's pitch black down here,' I protested anxiously, and was not surprised when his stride did not slow down one bit, as if he possessed cat eyes. And so I found myself walking through absolute darkness with my soul mate terrified of all the unseen threats surrounding me. I jog on this trail three times a week in the morning; it is a whole different universe at night. My body was tense against his as I resisted our swift pace into the dark depths of the unknown, a description as trite as the irrational fear that paralyzed me. As though we had literally entered the darkness of the subconscious mind, I was afraid there was a serial killer hiding behind every ghostly gray tree trunk. Yet there was nothing to be afraid of except all my own amorphous fears, which not even my Master's strong, confident presence could completely dispel. Gradually, my eyes adjusted somewhat and I was able to make out the edge of the path and the silhouettes of trees, and yet everything surrounding me – all of soulless nature itself – continued feeling like a threat to my brain, addicted to light and reason. It wasn't until Master commanded me to pull down my pants and panties and brace myself against a tree that a semblance of peace and calm possessed me despite my wind-thrashed hair and the nerve-wracking amorphous ground across which I had to tread to get to the trunk. When he penetrated me roughly from behind, all my fears vanished; I felt vulnerable in a completely different way, desirable, yielding but strong, utterly complete. Filled with my Master's erection my sensuality felt invigoratingly one with the sedate but also passionately alive forest around us, our love the natural pulsing heart of the darkness. He climaxed deep inside me, and suddenly it began raining in deafening, drenching waves that made me laugh because now I was wet both inside and out, not to mention figuratively drowning in the love I felt for this man who always gently but relentlessly pushed me beyond my self-imposed limits, enabling us to enjoy new experiences and adventures that always brought us sensually and spiritually closer together. My pants weighed ten times more by the time we got home, but I felt wonderfully light-hearted from our sojourn out in the stormy darkness.

We made the best of Hurricane Isabel, my middle name. In the dead of night the power went out. Red and green lights began flashing around the house, digital clocks all announcing it was twelve-o'clock as if in the grip of a perverse enchantment. The thunder didn't wake me up; it was Merlin crawling up to my face in bed; unlike his mythical namesake, he's terrified of lightning. I had already equipped our bathrooms with candles and we had a gas stove. My only concern was all the food in my refrigerator and freezer, not to mention my chest freezer. So in the morning, Master and I went on a quest for breakfast and ice, none of which were easy to find. Isabel had come and gone, leaving a stunned community in her wake. It was a small miracle when we at last found bags of ice in a dark supermarket miles from home. The contents of my freezers safe for the time being, we proceeded to enjoy the temporary absence of technology – computers, television, stereos, etc. – sitting out on the porch listening to a battery powered radio while we talked. Later in the day, we sipped Stinger's perfect Vodka Martinis playing cards and still talking. It was wonderful being pushed into each other's arms like that without any distractions whatsoever, and Merlin thoroughly enjoyed himself as well looking down at the trees and the street. I was almost disappointed when the power surged back, and once more I had to share Master with our electronic harem; nevertheless, I was also relieved, because if there's one thing I can't be happy without for long is air conditioning, and I enjoy technological toys as much as he does. In our free time, Master and I enjoy doing almost everything together. I don't understand couples who take separate vacations, or the concept of 'girl's night out' which makes no sense to me since I only went out with girls to look for the right man to be alone with!

* * *

I think one of the truest sayings out there is, 'You can't please everyone' and also true is that many people don't even know how to please themselves. A child of the twentieth century is in many ways brought up divorced from his true nature, and how not when the earth – the soul's manifest reflection – is being systematically raped and destroyed under our very noses without us even noticing since we don't feel the loss as part of us; as really affecting us. It's not surprising that a woman who is now happily a Masterful man's love slave would not have hesitated to do drugs when she was younger and desperately searching for a ticket out of her soul's rational blues. Loving my Master, being with my Master, living with my Master and writing – exercising my extrasensory faculties of love and creativity every day and every night – are having the same natural, gradual effect on my senses and perceptions as acid once had in a more superficial way. If I had not experienced acid's magical kiss on my brain, it would have been even more difficult for my soul to break out of the rational chains in which it was raised; isolated from my true sensual nature, imprisoned in the cell of my gray matter with two barred windows, one looking out on the romantic past, the other at a universe of stars and an endless possibility of other worlds – our only hope on a dying planet. But where there is life there is still hope, right? So I choose to believe, because a positive outlook is the vital ring on which hang all the keys freeing me from the limits of my gray matter – imagination, metaphor, poetry, art and religion, science and discovery, faith and fascination, the list goes on... and I can't help but feel they all mysteriously penetrate the seemingly empty keyhole of a divine love.

A third excerpt from the illuminated manuscript of my own personal Dark Ages:

Eric, a cute young Canadian, introduced me to acid. I recall putting the tiny, square piece of paper on my tongue about half-an-hour before going to the bathroom at Fun Place, its grey dungeon-like atmosphere the prison of my normal, limited perceptions from which I'd soon be released. I couldn't imagine what was in store for me, I just knew that I was more than ready for it, smiling at my flushed face in the mirror before running out to the car where Eric, Lourdes and her date, John, were waiting. I was the only one on acid.

I had always mentally believed in the divine unity of everything, but that night tripping in Tropical Park, I actually experienced a beatific sense of wholeness that I didn't have to make any effort to defend from my reason; the drug's energy destroyed all doubt-crawling thoughts like a laser beam. I felt as though I had become my real self.

'It's all so simple!' I flung my arms around Eric's neck, an action I kept repeating because our embrace was the very core of the night to which I naturally returned as the tide ebbs and flows. I'd run off and enjoy the playground, or skip down the path as if it was the yellow brick road, then fly back to rest against his chest and feel his arms around me as the whole marvelous world. 'It's so simple I!' I kept repeating. 'Why, *how*, have they complicated it so much?' Really, I could not for the life of me understand how mankind had managed to fuck life up so badly when it was divinely simple.

I saw a Volkswagen with ears and a tail attached to it, and I couldn't stop laughing for a long time it seemed such a perfect symbol of how ridiculous modern man was, driving a mouse around, vitally a coward inside despite all his superficial sophistication. As we walked through the vast park, deserted at that time of night, I was torn between Eric's golden-haired, smiling warmth and a deep, deep love for my shadow. There were no words to describe it. I just knew it was the real me. 'I should always think like my shadow,' I thought. 'It is absolutely pure and free and fearless, and it's me, the *real* me.' I could ignore my jeans, sagging like old flesh, and my earth-brown boots, because I was really that slender darkness dancing on the grass with no worries, no problems; no paranoia's.

Lourdes had taken two metha-qualudes, so we were on the opposite ends of reality. If it had been a game of see-saw I would have been laughing high in the sky as she sat with her ass flat on the ground. I looked into the car, grinning from ear to ear, and when I saw she was studying her report card, sleepily wondering where the hell that one 'D' had come from, it was too much for me; Eric had to lead me to the calm, luminous beauty of water so I could stop laughing. The tall, thick blades of grass rising from the lake reminded me of the columns of an ancient temple, so that I knew why I had always loved the pre-Christian world so much, filling notebook after notebook with facts I intended to use when I wrote novels set in the long-ago past. Humanity in its youth had perceived reality the way I did when I was tripping, as absolutely magical. The deep water universe gave birth to galaxies of light when I threw in a stone and made a wish, my heart sinking just a little when nothing happened. Yet I knew all I hoped and desired would eventually flow to me if I really believed it was possible.

After forever, Eric drove us home, waiting inside the softly purring car until we were safely inside the house. I looked back at this haunting creature in my driveway, shining and black with two intense, beautiful stars at its head, and my wooden front door was impressive as a castle drawbridge. Lourdes dove straight into bed but I remained in the living room, where a part of me started to panic as I watched the walls breathing. Mami's portrait was alive, which made me worry she wasn't anymore, and I actually opened the door to her room to make sure she was sleeping safely. Then I sat down in a chair and felt the endless darkness all around us, our cozy house a tiny, powerless matchbox in a cold, endless darkness…

Eventually I was able to fall asleep, and in the lovely, reassuring light of day I remembered only the beatific feeling of wholeness with the world and my love for my shadow. On another occasion, Eric and I drove down to Key Biscayne, parked my car right in front of the water, and lay on my hood staring up at the moon, soft, dark clouds wafting around it like furs slipping off a woman's smooth, white shoulder. My breathing and the rhythm of the tide were one and unconfined to my flesh, the living space of my chest extending up to the heavens. The whole world had become my body. Eric massaged my shoulders and back, the pressure of his fingers causing three-dimensional images to flash on my closed eyelids in little multiple squares that advanced then receded to be replaced by another web of vivid images. Pictures flared out of the tension in my muscles, coils of energy unwound by the pressure of his touch.

We leaned against the car kissing. I was wearing a long

necklace hung with little golden fish, and I dangled it in front of him teasingly. 'These are the keys to the kingdom,' I said, caressing the divinely warm temple column of his neck. 'Will you come with me?'

'Sure.' He pressed his body against mine, staring into my eyes. 'Let's go.'

On another night Lourdes, her lover, Lori, Alley-cat, me, and another girl whose name I've forgotten, each took a hit of acid and drove to *Finders Lounge*, a live music club beside the ocean. We walked along the sand for a while, leaving the club behind us.

On our left rose the lights of hotels and buildings like the glimmering scales of a Chinese Dragon coiling and uncoiling in golden trails, filling the heavens with vivid, oriental colors. I wondered why I was seeing the lights of the city as the cold scales of an elaborate reptile... because they were temples built to the coiling serpent of the dollar sign, money swallowing all true, living values and making everything flow with a bloodless, heartless ease as long as you possess a lot of it. But the roaring rhythm of the tide was *not* the financial demon's breath; the soft sucking sand was not its flesh. The city swirling around me as I turned was like a huge roulette wheel reducing the stars to the meaningless dice of coincidence – whether you have a good life or a bad life, whether you're happy or not, is all just a matter of chance, not a divine hand.

The sight of the city distressed me so much I couldn't stop thinking about mami and my brother and how upset they would be if they knew I did acid. This thought was like an anchor bringing me down, hooking itself between my eyes so

I wasn't free to glide way on the sensuality of the night's experience. I was docked to sadness, uncertainty and fear wondering why I couldn't share this intensity with those I love most dearly. I had to force myself to turn away from this state of mind just as I had from the cold force of the city, taking pleasure and strength from Alley-cat's calmly smiling presence as we crouched together on the sand and gazed out at the dark, breathing body of the ocean. Then all five of us formed a circle to protect our joint from the wind, huddling together like football players thinking up strategy. Laughing, we entwined arms and legs until we couldn't tell where one of us ended and the other began.

'Wait, is this my arm?'

'Hey, where's my leg... oh, there it is!'

Laughter, warmth, perfect security, we were one body and one being enigmatically composed of individuals enjoying this sense of union, the burning joint we were passing like a tiny lighthouse in the vast darkness. With the ocean sounding as if it was coming closer and closer, breaking right at our feet, I felt we were a primitive life-form just emerged from the salty depths. Then suddenly the cocoon broke up and countless Millenniums passed in a matter of seconds; the fact that everyone was walking back towards the club seemed an absolute impossibility.

'Hey, wait a minute,' I cried. 'I need a few thousand years to get ready!' In the blink of an eye we had gone from being a sing celled organism clinging to a rock by the primeval ocean into two-legged, two-armed, two-eyed young women, all in the timeless space of what felt like an eternal night. What did I look like now that I wasn't a single cell in a communal body?

'Alley-cat, do I look okay?' I asked. Lourdes and I stood close together; our sibling bond was strong when we were tripping, mysteriously feeling how the same genes had formed us.

'Are you kidding? I'm honored to trip with people who look like you two!' Her eyes were so wide I got a reassuring sense of how beautiful I apparently was.

Inside the club everyone went their own way and I found myself staring at a guy's neck as if it was a luscious tropical island in the midst of the club's dark and seemingly bottomless waves. He was wearing a golden axe earring, his black hair falling over his pale flesh, and I found myself standing beside him at the bar. We started talking, and the next thing I knew we were out in the parking lot leaning against his red car, then sitting inside it making out. I had to control myself, because I could have devoured him without the slightest effort, or so I felt as I bit his neck with the desire to make its deliciousness somehow part of me. His sex didn't interest me because I didn't love him; it was mysteriously through his neck that we could relate purely as warm life-form to life-form. In his cock lay his personality, through which I would uncomfortably get to know all our current vital differences. At one point I glanced into the back seat, and couldn't stop laughing at the picture of the Soviet Leader, who had just recently died, laid out in state. 'His head looks just like a cabbage!'

CHAPTER EIGHT

Pussy Magic

My website seems to attract male photographers; several of them have written to me expressing the desire to photograph me, either clothed or unclothed, or both. I'm flattered, because so far the men who have approached me are all quite talented; nevertheless, I prefer self-portraits or having Master take pictures of me. One such visual suitor intrigued me more than the others, perhaps because he was of Egyptian origin and ancient Egypt has always fascinated me. From his e-mails I got the impression he could perhaps become my friend, and Master gave me permission to arrange meeting him for a drink one evening. I must admit, I've always been a touch naïve – I'm invariably ready to believe the best about people until they disappoint me – but this is no longer a danger now that I have my Master to protect me. So we met this photographer – whom I will name Remy – at a restaurant in Arlington. He was pleasant enough, and I liked his shaved head and the general cast of his features, reminiscent of an ancient Egyptian scribe, but his aura did not send any significant electricity through mine when he first walked up to us where we were sitting at the bar, and even though I found elements of his conversation interesting, I was not challenged or intrigued by him. I knew right away we weren't destined to be friends, but when he invited us over to his home one night for dinner, Master gave me permission to accept the invitation, which I did thinking there was the slight possibility Remy would reveal more interesting dimensions in private. I was also still considering allowing him to photograph me if I liked what I saw of his work enough to inspire me to pose for him.

Remy was the perfect host; he even let us bring Merlin. His small garden apartment was cozy, and as sensually inviting as a tent in a desert oasis, western couches and chairs replaced by leather footstools embroidered with gilded thread, and a large elevated space covered with colorful oriental rugs (which also decorated the walls) and strewn with pillows. We had brought a bottle of wine with us as an offering, but Remy had his own vintage he wanted to share with us which accompanied a light but delicious dinner of grilled chicken breast with a special sauce served on a bed of gourmet greens. There was a selection of CD's rotating in the player, and the front door was open to the yard, enabling us to enjoy the changes of light and temperature as the sun set and day smoothly flowed into night. I was of two minds when our host brought out a water pipe. There was a time in my life when I couldn't even think of living without marijuana, but ever since I met my Master I rarely ever indulge in the substance; I don't need it or want it anymore. However, I make it a point to allow myself to be wicked on special occasions, and even Merlin took an innocent hit of the pungent herb.

I was wearing a form-fitting black skirt made of faux leather in the front of supple cloth in the back, a tight black sleeveless shirt decorated with a series of looped chains in front, black high-heeled sandals, and my black leather collar. I don't remember if Master commanded me to dance for them or if I rose from the sand-soft cushions of my own volition, following the irresistible current of the music. I was feeling intensely relaxed and sensual in the presence of two men who obviously thought I was beautiful and desired me. I had never been alone like this with two men before, and it was exciting because one of them was my beloved Master – a magical fact that turns whatever circumstances we find ourselves living into an adventure from which we can both walk away if it ceases to be pleasurable, or as soon as we tire of it. I love to dance, and judging from the look in Master's and Remy's eyes, they loved watching me perform for them. I was thrilled to be the center of attention with no other woman present competing with me, and I did not hesitate to obey when Master commanded me to pull my shirt up and show them my breasts. I was inspired, and perspiring, as I danced, and it felt wonderful pulling the constricting cloth up against my chest to expose more of my skin to the cool air conditioning. By now the front door was closed for privacy.

'Isn't she cute when she's all worked up?' Master asked.

Remy's smile deepened, 'Oh, yes…'

I made myself comfortable on the carpet between Master's knees where he sat on a gilded footstool. I was facing away from him as his hands fondled my breasts, my legs wantonly spread and one of my knees bent. I was deliberately teasing Remy with a possible glimpse of my pussy as he returned from the kitchen carrying a bowl of fruit mixed with their own juices. I had made it clear to Master in private asides when our host was temporarily out of earshot that I was not sexually attracted to him, in fact, his submissiveness turned me off. But I knew it was pleasing my Master to show me off as he enjoyed the feeling of another man desperately desiring what was his, and I was high enough to indulge in the entertaining fantasy of Remy as an ancient Egyptian slave boy, especially when he began serving both my Master and me fruit from the bowl with his fingers. I smiled up at Master, who smiled down into my upturned face, both of us delighted by the harmless sensual game. It became a bit more serious when I found myself no longer able to resist the ancient Egyptian appeal of Remy's sensually smiling mouth and asked Master for permission to kiss him.

'You want to kiss him, Missa?'

'Yes, Master, may I?'

'Yes, you may, Missa.'

I made sure Remy was in the right position to give Master a good view of my lips meeting and parting against those of another man, and I must say the kiss was lingering and sweet; lovely indeed. Our handsome slave boy was a sensitive artist possessed of a very talented tongue.

'May I kiss her breasts?' It was Remy's turn to ask for permission, and Master smilingly nodded his ascent.

The chains attached to my shirt (which was still bunched up against my chest) were draped over and around my breasts, and the touch of cool hard metal contrasting with Remy's warm soft tongue was delicious. It was inevitable he would ask Master for permission to lick my pussy, and the eloquent attention of his mouth savoring my nipples was making me more than amenable to the idea.

'Do you think I should let him lick your pussy, Missa?' Master asked me.

I didn't think it was a trick question; I knew he would enjoy watching another man kiss my sex lips, and that he wouldn't be jealous if I expressed the desire to experience the sensation. 'I don't see how it could hurt,' I replied, and Remy's smile deepened as he slowly crouched before me, relishing the anticipation a few seconds longer before he gently buried his head between my legs. He went down on me for a long, long time, occasionally taking another hit from the pipe or pausing to sip his wine before resuming his ardent oral devotions. As another man worked to pleasure me, Master held me against him, his jean-clad legs on either side of me the columns of my own personal temple. I couldn't look up at his face, but I could toss my head back and suck on the hard fingers he slipped into my mouth as Remy's tongue danced in and out of my cunt; sucking up the dewy juices of my labia and circling my clitoris like a predator surrounding its prey patiently waiting to move in for the kill.

'You're so delicious,' he whispered, glancing up at me with soulfully dark eyes and a luminous smile that transported me back in time... I was a queen enjoying the ministrations of her worshipful attendant...

He kept eating me, licking me and sucking me, and gently (too gently for my taste) fingering my slick depths, doing his absolute best to make me come, and even though the experience was nothing but pleasurable, I soon found myself growing bored. Gazing down at his smoothly shaved head working between my thighs, I distinctly felt my soul residing deep inside the sensual shrine of my pussy. He was doing his best to seduce me, to lure my soul out in the form of a climax, but he was wasting his time. Skill is not enough; my soul only responds to Stinger's. I tried glancing up at him Master again, wondering if he'd had enough of this little erotic scene and hoping he would end it soon. I was beginning to feel sorry for Remy, who was still moaning and smiling with pleasure, but I sensed he was also just a bit upset that all his talent was not having the desired effect on me. I was happy when the next time he took a break, Master announced it was time we were leaving soon.

Remy did his best to keep us there longer, and of all the photographs he showed us, my favorite was a mysterious close-up of a woman's stocking-clad thighs and pussy evoking the entrance to a dark, cave-like shrine... in which my orgasm had remained stubbornly buried despite all his best efforts. It was only the fact that my Master was there, taking pleasure in sharing his wealth, and in penetrating my mouth as another man's tongue thrust into my pussy, that turned me on.

Remy continued e-mailing me for a while, but I never responded. He was an actor in a one-night play Master and I enjoyed in a fashion, but we had no desire to repeat that particular performance. I like my men absolutely straight and dominant; submissive slave boys are not to taste, but I was glad to have had the opportunity to prove that to myself by way of actual experience.

Master asked me the other day, 'Do we need to invite a slave boy over to give you a foot rub?' teasingly reminding me of our night with Remy.

Much as I love having any part of my body massaged, I wrinkled my nose in distaste and shook my head. 'No thanks,' I said.

* * *

Shortly after he collared me, Master commanded me to begin doing Kegal exercises to strengthen my vaginal muscles. I did as he said, exhilarated by my increasing awareness of this mysterious part of my body I had believed was essentially beyond my control; hidden, secret and passive. I was wrong. Now every time I experience the pleasure of Master's cock in my pussy, I consciously caress and squeeze him with my innermost flesh, an exercise that tugs on the lips of my sex and directly stimulates my clitoris. I have not yet succeeded in coming without touching myself, but I do sense it's possible for me, which is saying a lot. The stronger my abdominal and vaginal muscles become, the tighter I feel inside, which makes Master's penetrations even more intensely pleasurable. And somehow the better shape the muscles of my pelvis are in, the easier it is for me to relax and allow him to thrust deeper and harder and faster as my clit quivers like a divine drop of dew on the petals of my labia, shimmering with the luminous possibility of a climax.

I remember the night when I made the subtle but hauntingly effective transition from mere Kegal calisthenics to what I call Pussy Magic, because that's what is, and it really works. Master was fucking me from behind, and with my eyes closed, I saw an ideal image of my body and his hard-on driving in and out of it; I visualized his erection sliding in and out of my pussy, and imagined what it was feeling inside me… and then I wasn't just imagining or visualizing the sensations his cock was experiencing, I was 'telling' it what to feel; I knew it was feeling what I wanted it to feel as my innermost flesh mysteriously shaped itself to the will of my desires, becoming ideally slick and tight and perfectly stimulating. I could even sense the subtle tightening of my hole just where it opens up to my cervix squeezing his thrusting head with an irresistible rhythm that made him come amazingly fast.

'Very good, Missa,' he said breathlessly, and I knew I was right – what I had just done was a physiological reality not merely an erotic fantasy. The next day I wrote in my journal:

Pussy Magic really works! I project this image of my body and imagine his penis going into it, and the perfection of the experience, and it works. He feels it, and I feel that way – beautiful, sensual, a perfectly fine-tuned instrument of pleasure. This image projection – where I imagine what his penis is penetrating and feeling – really works! I visualize my body as ideally fuckable, I really believe in – I embody – the intense desirability of my beauty, and I see the full length of his cock driving into my body, which I position in just the right way to receive him; I see my innermost flesh gripping and caressing every inch of his erection in all the right places, and it works!

As always, I seek to express everything I'm feeling and experiencing with Master in my erotic romances, so that in a sense there is nothing fictional about them. The following are excerpts from my latest novel, *The Fabric of Love*, expressing how I feel about pussy magic:

'Arch your back.' His hand pressing down on the base of her spine, he penetrates her.

His thrust has the rending effect of a weapon at the angle she is offering her pussy to him. 'Oh, God, Master!' Under the circumstances it feels perfectly natural to be calling him that because at the moment he has complete mastery of her flesh. Even though his erection is only coming into contact with her vaginal walls, it feels as though he is stabbing himself to the very core of her physical being. The intensity of the experience makes up for the slight discomfort; her pussy has never felt so open and so tight at the same time, and she can sense how good her tight slot feels to his hard-on – slick and soft and deep and clinging, the cushion of her cervix kissing his head and welcoming him into a hot, wet harem of sensations as she consciously milks him, tightening and relaxing around him.

'Oh, yes,' he whispers, and a profound triumph deepens her cunt's ability to absorb his relentless strokes as she suddenly (more with the combined power of her senses than her mind) becomes aware of just how much power she actually has over him even in her vulnerable position. Closing her eyes, she clamps her pussy muscles around his erection, squeezing him gently at first and then harder and harder, until it's as if there is no limit to how tightly she can grip him. Her sex is a cosmic black hole sucking him into the ever diminishing singularity of her innermost being, and the bigger and thicker his penis gets, the closer he comes to the event horizon of his pleasure, the more she tightens her hold on him. In her mind's eye she can see the shape and length of his cock wrapped in her hot flesh. No other man has ever inspired her to such visualizations before, much less filled her with the mysterious ability to tighten endlessly around him. She knows when he starts coming because of the quiet, breathless sounds he makes and because he gets so hard she almost can't stand how good his increasingly violent penetrations feel.

'Oh, Mira…'

She cries out in triumph and pleasure as her awareness of everything is momentarily laid waist by the explosion of his pleasure deep in her sex. His throbbing cock fills her almost to bursting as she relishes the sinful baptism of his cum drenching her insides…

…She has been fantasizing about this position and this cross ever since she saw it; however, she couldn't have imagined the intense gratification of his hands parting her ass cheeks so he could thrust his tongue up into her pussy from behind. His skilled oral devotion comes as a blessing to her overwrought senses. She is deliciously aware of her lush labial lips as he takes them in his mouth, alternately sucking and feasting on the sweet and tender crack in her flesh. Tendrils of pleasure indistinguishable from pure, hot energy are slowly unraveling deep in her pelvis, snaking down to meet the tip of his licking, flicking, thrusting tongue, and the subtle, exquisite conflagration is concentrated in her swelling clitoris. Everything is so hard – his fingers digging into her nether cheeks, the wood pressing against her nipples and belly, the stiff leather cuffing her wrists and ankles – and she is so soft and yielding and helpless.

'Oh, Master, please, please…'

He shoves his face into her vulva with a ravenous growl.

'Oh, God, please fuck me, Master, please!'

His features cease to imprint themselves on the haunting clay of her hotly juicing sex. 'I suppose I could do that,' he says. And he does.

Being nailed to the cross takes on a whole different meaning to the Catholic school girl inside Mira. Her breasts are no longer crushed against the wood because they're in his hands, his fingers pressing cruelly into her tender mounds. He braces himself on their soft fullness as his cock surges into her cunt over and over again in a tight, pounding rhythm. It seems to Mira that her whole life was leading up to these moments when absolute fulfillment pushes all the thoughts out of her head. She is at peace as she never has been before and not despite the violence trapped between her thighs but precisely because of it. No man has ever fucked her so selfishly. No man has ever banged her from behind when she was bound and helpless to defend herself. No man has ever driven his erection so deep into her pussy. He stabs her with increasing force in between pausing to circle his hips and grind against her ass cheeks, forcing her to savor the sensation of his hard-on packed into her hole; intensifying her awareness of his cock remorselessly rammed up into her body as he stirs her juices up with spiraling motions, making a hot cauldron of her cunt. The darkness behind her blindfold is black magic – a staggeringly powerful spell is being worked by the controlled confines of her limbs and senses and transforming her into the pure, unresisting vessel of his pleasure. Her sex, her breasts, her legs, her ass, her neck, all of her was designed with his lust in mind. Ground into the palms of his hands, her nipples are hard as diamonds refracting pricelessly sharp sensations through her flesh as his penis seems to drive deeper and deeper into her pelvis. He flings her hair over one shoulder and bites her neck with such vicious abandon that she grows limp as prey in a predator's jaws, allowing herself to be absolutely possessed and loving it even as she marvels at the paradox that his giving no thought to her comfort and pleasure pleases her more than anything.

He comes inside her with a vengeance, as if drowning all evidence of any man who has been there before him. Afterwards, he remains buried inside her, the weight of his body pressing her against the cross, and she is so stunned and fulfilled she is glad of its support. Surely this was the climax of her first test as a sex slave. She hopes it was because her senses and emotions are completely spent for the moment, as spent as his penis, also only for the moment, thank the Lord.

* * *

One stormy night, I stripped naked, slipped on my black leather collar and black six-inch heels, and waited for Master to find me on his bed like that. He was working in the study, but I imagined he would wonder where I was after a while and come looking for me. In the meantime, I lay languidly listening to the thunder, which began to feel like my own soul purring – the sound of the profound pleasure I took in being my Master's slave filling the universe. And while my body waited for him, the storm seemed to be making love to me… I gasped as though suddenly penetrated by unseen forces when lightning struck so close it blew the lights and the phone. When Master still didn't appear, I got up off his waterbed, and crawled on my hands and knees into the study. He glanced over, saw me, and watched my cat-like approach towards his chair with a serious expression in his eyes. He stroked my hair gently, and told me to go prepare myself for anal training. We still call it that even though I have long since graduated – Master can fuck my ass whenever he wants to as hard as he wants to without any preparation except for a bit of KY Jelly. This was not the case in the beginning, when my sphincter needed to be slowly coaxed into opening up, and often painfully resisted the thick, hard length of his erection pushing through my tight ring like a god's finger forcing the marriage of our flesh in an excruciatingly unnatural way. Now all I experience is a fulfillment so intense my mouth gapes open hungry for his fingers or his tongue or the fantasy of another cock so that I'm gloriously filled up at both ends. And if I also had another penis or a dildo stretching my pussy open around it, making my backdoor even more deliciously tight for Master, all the better. I love the fact that I can let him fuck my ass as hard as he fucks my cunt and that it turns me on so much.

I was awarded what we jokingly term my 'Anal PhD' one Saturday night. We were sitting naked on our black leather couch sipping Master's transcendent Vodka Martinis, and both of us seriously needed to pee, but suddenly he said, 'Take off your clothes and bring me the KY' ignoring my desperate protests. He almost literally dragged be into my bathroom, and then pulled me into the tub with him, where he commanded me to pee as he proceeded to fuck my ass with a vengeance. But it was like trying to pee in a dream; I couldn't do it. He really fucked my ass that night, pulling me hard up against him and fondling my breasts; reaming me with an unrestrained force that had me crying out with surprise and from the almost unbearable pleasure. Finally, he had mercy on me. Pulling his erection out of my tight hole, he told me to kneel before him and relieve myself. I obeyed him gratefully, moaning with mingled dread and desire as I stood up on shaky legs and he turned me around to continue fucking my ass. At one point I was bent completely forward, bracing myself on the floor of the tub with my fingertips as he used my anus harder than ever. Then he led me into the bedroom, where he once again thrust his hard-on through my blazing ring as I crouched on the bed in the sleen position. I loved every second of his almost brutal assault on my sphincter, but at one point I knew I couldn't take much more and breathlessly begged him to come. 'You're going to come for me *now*,' I gasped, squeezing his thrusting cock with my rectal muscles, and he did indeed come, devastatingly. Afterwards, he led me more gently into his bathroom, where we laughingly decried I had just received my anal PhD as he made me kneel in the tub so he could pee all over me, even into my mouth, although this time I didn't swallow his clear, almost sweet-tasting urine. Then we rinsed off together, and later I wrote in my journal, 'That was the best Martini Saturday ever!' The next day we were *so* relaxed, and muscles in my legs and arms ached in a delicious way, muscles I hadn't even know were there. My anus didn't feel sore until forty-eight hours later, burning a little when I went to the bathroom, but not much, and a little Vaseline cream took care of that.

Anal sex cannot be forced our faked; I prefer not to have any other man in my ass except my Master during a double penetration.

I never would have believed myself capable of enjoying Golden Rain or Water Sports or whatever you want to call it, but I should have known I would love every part of my Master and everything he did to me, including his urine and the occasional times he empties himself directly into my mouth. He had peed all over my body once as I knelt in the tub, but he had avoided any contact with my face, so it was a shock when one night he commanded me to kneel in his bathtub and to open my mouth as he positioned the head of his cock directly in front of my face. I whined and protested, hurt and appalled that he wanted to humiliate me in that way, but he was firm about his desire to relieve himself between my lips, and I have never been able to resist doing whatever he wants me to. So he peed in my mouth, and I held his piss before spitting it out as he continued peeing all over my naked body, filling my mouth two or three more times in the process. Then he stepped into the tub with me, and fucked my pussy from behind for a while before making me kneel before him again so he could ejaculate all over my face. And I loved it all, especially the way we laughed together afterwards feeling so intimate and happy. Later on when we were watching TV on the couch, Master told me peeing into my mouth, and then coming all over my face, had been very relaxing for him, and I was totally content.

On another Martini Saturday, while we were watching *Farscape* or *Babylon 5* (we love good science fiction) Master remarked that he had to pee, but didn't get up to do so.

Part of me grudgingly resisted the hint, yet after only a minute or two I heard myself say, 'Would you like to pee in my mouth, Master?'

'I was waiting for you to offer, Missa,' he replied, smiling with pleasure that I had done so. Then I surprised us both by kneeling right there in front of him on the rug instead of following him to a bathroom. I actually swallowed his offering twice, and I would have swallowed it all if he had commanded me to, but he didn't; he finished peeing in the toilet while I held his erection, learning how to direct it and not to squeeze it too tightly.

Some time after that, I wrote in my journal:

Well, I went all the way with the Golden Rain last night and swallowed the full load, and I took it to this next natural step myself, because he had commanded me merely to take a mouthful and let it go in the toilet, but I was kneeling on the floor in the living room and it seemed more work to get up and walk to the bathroom – it seemed like a lame thing for a truly devoted slave to do, to get up and not take it all, so I did, which very much surprised and pleased him. And it didn't taste bad at all.

Needless to say, I would never consider letting someone else piss all over me, much less even think about swallowing their urine. As John said, 'It's an act of love' and Master is the only one who can baptize me and give me communion in this way.

* * *

Before I met Master, I could count on one hand how many times a man had been able to bring me to orgasm just with his fingers and his mouth. I have since lost track of how many times an indescribable pleasure has flowed between my Master's lips with mysterious, almost haunting eloquence... I sometimes have 'visions' while he is going down on me that stoke my ecstasy with a timeless eroticism our two bodies are only a part of like two unique drops of salty water in a boundless sea of sensuality. On a hotel bed in Toronto – where we spent a wonderfully relaxing hedonist week at the *Fairmont Royal York* – on two different lazy afternoons, Master went down on me. The sun was shining into our fifteenth floor room, but with my eyes closed I was back in a monastery cathedral in Portugal we had visited the year before… I was lying helplessly on the slab of a sarcophagus on an overcast and chilly evening while a priest devoured my innocent pussy as I writhed against the cold stone willingly sacrificing my soul to the sinful pleasure…

On the second luminous afternoon, when my Master knelt between my legs where they hung comfortably off the edge of the king size bed, the mood of my fantasy was completely different… this time my skin, which was smooth and golden from a day spent on a nude beach out on the lake, belonged to a woman in ancient India, and both my Master and I were figures from a Tantric temple come to life, especially after he made me climax and then climbed onto the bed to make love to me, his long dark hair flowing down his back as he smiled down into my eyes …

When my Master worships my pussy with his lips, tongue and fingers, it feels better than anything else on earth, and one night, he tied me to the big green chair in our living room, turned off all the lights, lit a fire along with some candles, turned on some soft music, and went down on me for well over an hour; ninety minutes had passed according to the cable clock before he finally ceased sublimely torturing me; disciplining me with ecstasy, because even then he was teaching me a lesson – that my body truly is capable of constant pleasure and that only my mind limits the experiential horizons of my flesh. Small, whimpering sounds of disbelief and gratitude welled up from within me as he went down on me with a precision that was almost surgical in its power to cut through my defenses, yet there was nothing cold and passionless about his skill.

My pussy juiced helplessly as the tip of his tongue circled endlessly, making my clitoris feel like a priestess coaxed all the way out of her fleshly temple for the first time by the quality of devotion at last worthy of her sensitive spirit. In the past so many men simply attacked my clit with all the finesse of farmers trampling on a seed, expecting pleasure to naturally bloom between my thighs as a result. They sucked on my body's mysterious seed as though it was a simple sugar-based candy, making it defensively hard and producing the opposite effect of melting me in their mouth. A couple of my lovers were a bit more circumspect, but there was not enough passion in the almost mathematical application of licks, sucks, laps and nips they patiently subjected me to, seeking my sexual response like the answer to an almost impossibly complex equation.

As I hoped and suspected would be the case, being orally pleasured by a man felt stunningly different with my Master from the very beginning. When the muscle of his tongue works its way up between the folds of my labia, opening me up as he savors the nectar of my arousal, my back arches with longing; with the blind need to be penetrated by his cock or his tongue or his fingers, I don't care which, I just have to feel a part of him inside me before I completely lose my mind wanting him. Yet I have learned enough to know that pleading with him will only delay my fulfillment, so I submissively endure the divine torment of his mouth and fingers working my pussy up into a drenched frenzy that sucks him down to the very hilt of my incarnation when he finally penetrates me, but not after first subjecting me to a powerful climax. My nipples get so hard that when he reaches up and begins firmly stroking them between this thumb and forefinger a climax inevitably blooms between my thighs, my clit dissolving between his lips like a drop of dew reflecting all the heat of the sun. My brain can't seem to process the intensity of the orgasm that takes root in my pelvis and blossoms with devastating beauty in all my nerve-ends as I come in waves that just keep deepening and deepening rather than ebbing, my most vital muscles contracting as I cease to be aware of anything but a pure joy.

After he goes down on me, my Master always fucks me, and sometimes when he takes me from behind he rams his cock into my slick hole at an angle that leaves nothing to my imagination. If we're in the living room, the floor remorselessly hard beneath the area rug, I rest my cheek on it and clutch it to brace myself even as the rest of my body lies limp as a beached mermaid beneath his plunging dives. There is nothing passive about me on the inside, however; my pussy is actively, greedily grasping his erection, pulsing open and closed around him like a hungry anemone feasting on his totally fulfilling dimensions. He is so hard his relentless penetrations would almost hurt if my sex wasn't deliciously wet as he commands me to lie flat so he can spread his body on top of mine. The angle is excruciating, and I can't really handle it with a full bladder, otherwise I love how utterly helpless and submissive it makes me feel the more violently and selfishly he thrusts. I don't move a muscle, taking a perverse kinky thrill in playing dead, yet all the while I am engrossed in the profound pleasure of caressing and squeezing his cock with the most special muscles I possess. In my mind's eye I picture his erection stabbing me and visualize the walls of my innermost flesh wrapping around it, squeezing his shaft from the base to the head in a continuous rippling motion even as the rest of my flesh remains utterly submissive beneath him. I relish every second of his beating as he packs the full, rending length of his penis into my pussy with every stroke. And almost always I make him come inside me. I glory in making it impossible for him not to come. I am always determined to have the impenetrable darkness behind my eyelids illuminated by the exploding stars of his cum surging into my innermost space in an erotic Milky Way. I beg him to come silently, with the part of me made especially to coax everything I desire from a man. For years now I have been exercising my vaginal muscles, and my Master's breathless groans speak to the effectiveness of my self-training, as does the way his hard-on begins pulsing, further intensifying the pleasure bonding us, until I break my passive silence by crying out as his cock reaches critical mass and he ejaculates deep between my thighs.

CHAPTER NINE

Spiritual Hedonism

Master and I no longer live the hedonistically driven life we enjoyed our first year together in Miami when he first began training me as his slave and forcing me (with my full consent) to conquer a host of crippling fears and inhibitions. The pace of our relationship is different now, slower and more intimate as we become closer and closer and our love literally deepens with every passing day. In a sense when I look back on Miami it's as if we were living off the junk food of Swing clubs because we were so starved for erotic experiences we could share as we nourished pet fantasies and gave birth to even more desires we longed to fulfill together. We will soon be celebrating our third anniversary, and life just keeps getting better; a couple of less than satisfying experiences have helped us better define our sexual menu, and we have both the personal and financial power to entertain at home now, which can be a much more enjoyably prolonged and subtly intense experience than the fast-fun sex of Swing clubs. To me, Swing parties often feel like going back to preschool fully sexed. 'Oh, let's go play over here... Mm, that was fun, now let's go play over there...' It's not very focused and fulfilling, not to mention the utter absence of bondage & domination which adds a vital dimension to the experience as far as my own sexual arousal is concerned.

The muscle of fidelity in true love occasionally suffers a very painful spasm inside me akin to a spiritual Charlie horse as I prepare to use it in a whole different way, much more flexibly than I was taught to use it, before we play with other people. I still sometimes suffer an intense anxiety before swinging Master has to massage me through with his understanding, until I relax and understand again how different being in love and making love are from sex, because the truth is I crave sexual play, too. What I truly dread is the pornographic atmosphere of Swing clubs; if they were sacred temples, I would have no problem occasionally having sex with other people as part of our sensual communion with the world. Yet part of me can't help but be afraid of defying the laws of monogamy, it's like my fear of flying – I'm afraid I'll crash inside through jealousy or some other vital flaw in my lover's behavior equivalent to fatal engine failure. But I need to fly to go to exciting different places, and Swinging is necessary for the adventure of our sexuality, even though if the truth be told I think the fantasy of swinging and the memory of it are even more pleasurable than the actual experience. Our love is apart and beyond everything else.

Master and I exchanged these e-mails because I always need to tell him exactly how I feel about everything:

Master,

We mentioned that perhaps when we move to Louisiana we should just go the Swing Club in New Orleans and forget about trying to meet people online. Starz suddenly rearing its ugly head back into our lives has made me realize I don't really feel that way at all.

The way I feel (and I must always tell you how I feel, especially when the feelings are intense) is that a Swing Club is great for exhibi-

tionism and voyeurism, and sensual caressing of others, and maybe, just maybe, for meeting people we can see privately in the future. If we were to meet a couple you wanted us to play with in a Club, I would really appreciate it if we could actually talk with them first so they're aware the usual casual full swap (you with her, me with him) isn't an option.

I believe alt.com may prove much more fruitful in the vicinity of New Orleans, and I would like you to consider keeping our membership. Alt.com is good for screening people, letting them know just where we're coming from and what we will and won't do, and finding out about the nature of their desires, before we make the decision to be intimate with them. I know I've complained about wasting my time e-mailing people (and I'm sorry about that) but suddenly faced with the prospect of Starz again, I realize just how much more comfortable and relaxed I feel about the prospect of playing with people we have gotten to know to a certain extent. I think that, ultimately, this is a much more enjoyably controllable, not to mention hygienic, way to Swing.

Missa

Missa,

I'm glad that you wrote to me about this and I'm sorry to bring up issues for you again. You should know by now that exhibitionism and voyeurism, and sensual caressing of others, and maybe, just maybe, for meeting people we can see privately in the future is what I expect from a club visit. I don't know if alt.com itself will be very useful in

*LA but the idea is right and it or another venue might be. Certainly
I agree with your sentiments on this.*

Love you,
Stinger

One evening before the night a couple was coming over for drinks and appetizers and possibly more, depending on the chemistry between us, I shied away from my Master as he prepared to fuck me. 'I need to rest my orifices, Master,' I said, feeling like an athlete scheduled to run a marathon the next day.

'This is how we live our life, Missa,' he said with the tender concern I love and appreciate so much. 'When there's someone else here, great, but it's not something you need to worry about or prepare yourself for. I don't like you feeling all this pressure. There's no reason for you to feel pressured or afraid.'

'Yes, Master, but aren't you really excited about possibly enjoying two pussy's tomorrow night?'

'Yes, that will be fun, but mostly what pleases me is that it's all part of a beautiful continuum with you.'

Master and I invariably feel as though we've had our brains massaged after a night fucking around other people; after a night of watching other naked bodies make love and being watched, whether we come into sensual contact with them or not. We both feel that way after Swinging, and we both *need* to feel that way every now and then. It really is like a mysterious brain massage relaxing us on the most profound levels so that I am aware of the strangely tense state in which I live most of the time even though I consider myself less stressed than most people. For us Swinging is mostly about being together in public with other people like us;

actually having sex with other people there is rare, and that's fine with me. I've finally absorbed the truth of the fact that Master no more desires to sexually attack all the cute naked girls walking around Swing parties than I desire to pounce on all the handsome naked men.

We discovered a local group on yahoo called XOXO that was by invitation only. The idea behind it was one I could very much appreciate. Swing clubs can sometimes be a serious affront to one's aesthetic sense, and XOXO had taken matters into their own hands by holding a private party every month only attractive couples could attend. Membership in the group required a private invitation from other members, or you had to apply by sending pictures of yourself. Master and I promptly sent off our erotic application, and our acceptance arrived with flattering immediacy. That's how we found ourselves attending the next (and what turned out to be the last, although no one knew it at the time) party in D.C. at a place called *The House of Secrets*. The decor can only be described as an Art Deco horror film; nevertheless, it was a much more interesting venue than a regular club thanks mainly to its three floors reached by way of two long and steep staircases. My ass got the exercise of its life walking up and down the steps several times that night in six-inch high-heels. Ladies, who needs a gym, if you have a steep staircase in your house just walk up and down it thirty to forty times wearing six-inch heels and your ass will defy gravity till the day you die. For me the best thing about being at *The House of Secrets* is that I no longer had to be anxious about going there and could now look forward to leaving. Even when I was in my twenties I disliked going out late at night, not understanding why I had to wait until I was tired and felt like going to bed before I could leave the house to start having fun. Now that I'm older, I feel even more strongly about this. In my opinion, a Swing party should be held between two o'clock in the afternoon until around seven or eight o'clock at night, after which you can go out for a nice relaxing and nourishing dinner. My energy tends to peak in the afternoon, but I'll confess that once I was there and had sipped a little bit of vodka on ice I felt much better.

Going to any kind of club is not on my list of favorite things to do; there are many activities I enjoy infinitely more, such as taking Merlin for a walk; cooking and eating a gourmet meal; lying on the couch reading a good book; being flogged and fucked in the ass by my Master; having stimulating conversations; the list goes on. If it wasn't for Master there are many things I would never have done in my life, and would never continue doing, because in many ways I can be as passive as the moon; as dark and shy and introverted as a Lunar Maria gazing out into my own inner reality. Fortunately for me, I have been able to absorb my Master's strength and willpower and burning desire for experience by way of his direct commands, which are as inescapable as shafts of sunlight illuminating all the deepest, darkest recesses of my heart. Hence I have found myself in places like *The House of Secrets* where I didn't think I wanted to be even as I felt secretly happy to be there, once again traveling beyond my own mental and sensual horizons in my Master's utterly stimulating and perfectly safe company. I knew once we got there that nothing terrible was going to happen and that the next morning I was going to feel very relaxed and content and happy we had gone.

There is no place more comforting on earth than the side of my Master's neck. From the moment we arrived at our first XOXO party, I felt like a kinky Cinderella perversely looking forward to the time when the darkly enchanting sex slave in a tight black corset dress and extreme high-heels would turn back into the casually naked slave cuddling with her Master on the loveseat, her face buried in the warm and tender haven of his neck. But the evening had only just begun, and the first thing we did was explore this intriguing new venue from top to bottom. Downstairs consisted of two small bars and a dance floor. On the second floor there was a bathroom (that incidentally clogged up a couple of hours into the party forcing everyone into a very long line for the only other available toilet downstairs) a coat room and not much else. The supposed play areas were on the third floor – three rooms, none of which were furnished wiuth beds or mattresses. *The House of Secrets* was where rock stars and other artists partied after their performances; the place was not designed for Swingers in mind. There were lots of chairs and tables, and in the very back room – its intimate darkness spoiled by a porno film playing on the back wall – could be found the most comfortable seating in the house, but there was nowhere to get horizontal. We briefly talked to another couple downstairs on the dance floor, but everyone else seemed to know each other; they were all regulars in an off-premise D.C. club called *Entre Nous*. It was a little like being back in high school surrounded by cliques, but Master and I managed to enjoy ourselves together surrounded by other, I had to admit, refreshingly attractive naked people for a change. Upstairs, as if by unspoken consent, one of the rooms was filled with less decorative bodies, whereas the main play rooms were exclusively the domain of the more beautiful people. I had an orgasm riding my Master's cock, with a porno film playing behind me as he watched me, and the room, and anyone who might be watching us. I always enjoy being with my Master, but mostly I was bored. Ventilation was not the best in the most comfortable playroom, and after a while I was sick to death of girl-on-girl action on the screen, and no one was reaching out to touch someone. Nobody knew us, we didn't know them, and for the most part couples stayed together.

Towards the end of the night, Master and I found ourselves in a rather more public area where he made me sit naked on the edge of a chair with my legs spread as I displayed my pussy for all and sundry. I rather enjoyed the feel of him sitting behind me, tenderly but firmly supporting me as I assumed the regal, statuesque pose of a proud priestess of the Goddess wearing nothing but my jewelry and black vinyl high-heels. There was a handsome couple playing a few feet away and the girl was doing her best to embody the traditional blonde bimbo as her partner stuffed his cock into her mouth and down her throat as if she possessed no nerve-ends that could protest his rough, selfish use of her flesh. At least they were being passionate about it, in contrast to the clique of naked girls who walked into the room and sat down to smoke and chat, totally oblivious to and disinterested in the naked people seriously going at it around them. This didn't seem to bother Master in the least. He bent me forward at the waist so he could fuck me from behind, and to my surprise instead of needing to rest, my pussy responded by getting very wet. My sex experienced a much deeper pleasure than I had imagined possible, especially after hours of erotic stimulation. Instead of being worn out, my cunt felt perfectly primed, so that when Master commanded me to assume the sleen position on the carpet (made rather unappealing by it's a rough texture and discarded cigarette butts) I obeyed willingly. He gave me permission to touch myself, and while he banged me fervently from behind, and while the naked girls laughed and gabbed like plucked hens, I suffered an intense simultaneous orgasm with my Master in the most unlikely of circumstances. I was astonished, and very proud of myself. Master was also proud of me, but not astonished.

'We were together, Missa, it didn't matter where we were and who was there. I'm proud of you for being able to concentrate on us and our pleasure like that.'

As I've mentioned before, there's something very relaxing about watching other attractive naked bodies making love and to be two of those bodies. Master and I enjoyed our mysterious brain massage the next day as a result of our nocturnal activities, and I was happy we had gone to the XOXO party. Yet in my opinion once was enough in that particular venue; I was not looking forward to a repeat performance. I got my wish. Our first XOXO party turned out to be the last one held at *The House of Secrets*. Neighbors complained about noise emanating from the house (undoubtedly as a result of other parties) and XOXO was forced to look for another meeting place. It took them several months, and by then Master and I knew we were heading South, and therefore meeting a couple there we could play with in private had become rather a moot point; nevertheless, we were curious to see the new space and desired to once again socialize with the world in one of our favorite ways.

It turns out the most attractive Swingers of the D.C. metropolitan area were now to meet and mingle at a private house rented exclusively for the purpose. In my opinion the owners should have waited before they held the opening bash. The place had been hastily 'furnished' and was hardly inspiring – small bedrooms were covered with mattresses dressed in plain white sheets, the only décor consisted of candles threatening to light the gauzy curtains on fire, and to make matters truly resemble a Medieval painting of hell's lost souls writhing naked together in torment, the air-conditioning wasn't working properly. Imagine the accumulated body heat, and how much I sweat in my tight black vinyl dress. It was an almost orgasmic relief when Master unzipped it and freed my slick breasts. The house was not aesthetic, but it was small enough to force people to actually meet and talk to each other. We conversed with several couples, and I had more fun than at the first XOXO party because I got to kiss three different women, fondle two pairs of naked breasts, and I even got to spank a girl's ass. I love playing with another woman's body, especially if it doesn't lead to licking her pussy. I love watching other women being fucked while my Master is fucking me. I love coming into sensual contact with another couple while we're each making love to our partners. This position is not the best for my Master because he cannot see my face, but I really enjoy lying beneath another woman's breasts sucking on her nipples and fondling her soft tits while my Master fucks my pussy and her lover fucks her cunt from behind. I got to enjoy all that as well as the pleasure of sucking my Master's beautiful cock while people watched and commented to him on what a great ass I have. And in the end, the lack of proper air-conditioning afforded us an intensely sensual relief when Master and another man opened the window in one of the bedrooms. The cool caress of the strong breeze felt better to me than any other caress of the evening.

After the first XOXO party I wrote in my journal:

I had an orgasm in the back room riding Master's lap almost effortlessly, believing in my slenderness and beauty. Then I actually came with him in that public room full of chatting girls on the dirty carpet, against all odds, his second orgasm when he was fucking me from behind… his cock felt so good in my pussy, better and better as the night progressed. I think I was turned on by how he made me sit naked with my legs wide open exposed to everyone, at one time leaning against him while he played with my nipples.

* * *

I'm not just as Swinger, I'm a slave, and I need bondage, discipline, being restricted; being intensely stimulated on all levels of my sensual being not just in my sex. Master and I are planning to buy a house soon, which will enable us to create the bondage play room of our dreams and provide the stage where we can live out the drama of our love and sensuality both on our own and with the right players helping flesh out our deepest darkest fantasies in a safe, controlled environment. In this passage from my latest erotic romance, *The Fabric of Love*, I am fantasizing about one of the possible toys in our playroom:

She obeys him naturally, her pussy lips parting as if in wonder, and the slick sound her labial lips make as they open speaks loudly of unconfessed hungers. Suddenly, Mira realizes he is going to force the truth out of her, and that she won't be able to lie to herself or to the world anymore about the dark depths hibernating in her libido. She has never had her legs spread and suspended like this. The gynecologist's office was just a terrible tease that did not even hint at how gloriously vulnerable this position would make her feel. Her arms suffer the same fate as her legs, spread open over her head with her wrists resting in what feel like fur-lined straps he buckles just tightly enough that she can't wriggle her hands free. The final touch comes as a surprise. She gasps when her head is thrown back as he bends over to release a lever beneath the cushion. Immediately she worries that if he forces her to sustain this pose for too long the blood will rush to her head and she won't be able to bear it.

'Master…' she says, a tremor of uncertainty in her voice.

Darkness fills her vision as he comes and stands directly over her prone face. The universe is divided in half in his gleaming black thighs, and it feels like the hand of God descending over her features to gently caress her cheek and part her lips with the tip of his strong, demanding thumb.

'Mira, the first and the last and the most important lesson a slave has to learn is to trust her Master. You're worried I'll leave you like this for too long?'

'Yes, Master,' she admits, intensely grateful for his perceptive understanding.

'Very good, you were honest with me about it. But you came here of your own free will, Mira, which means you trust me. Yet clearly that trust still has its limits, and these limits are the only things in the room that are going to cause you pain and discomfort. There can be no limits to how much you trust me. The trust must be absolute and include the largest and smallest of your fears and anxieties.'

'Yes Master, I understand.' Her world is literally upside down. Pleasing him is all that matters to her now, and yet she knows that in doing so she will also mysteriously be fulfilling herself. This is the dance he mentioned, the beginning of the death spiral – the death of the doubts and fears limiting her experiences. She is in absolutely no physical danger, she knows this, yet being completely bound and helpless for the first time in her life is still an unnerving experience. Part of her is desperate to feel anxious. Another part of her is so excited she has to close her eyes as he cradles her head in both his hands and lifts it, stopping the flow of blood to her skull. He massages her scalp with his fingertips, and for an instant she can almost imagine she is at the beauty salon getting her hair washed, her head tilted back into the sink.

'Would you like to suck my cock?'

'Oh, yes, Master.'

He gently lets go of her head again, and she opens her eyes to try and get a glimpse of his penis as he unzips his tight pants. She needn't have worried. Soon his erection is all she can see, taste, smell and feel. He sinks to his knees and begins fucking her face. His hands caress her throat on the outside while the engorged head of his cock strokes it from the inside. Her wrists and ankles jerk in their straps in sympathy with her gag reflex, but whether she likes it or not the slender shaft of her neck remains completely open to him. The cool pillows of his balls press against her features in breathless contrast to his hard-on filling her mouth and throat like porous stone stiffening and swelling against her wet tongue. Dimly colorful lights flash behind her closed eyelids as the intoxicating smell and taste of him act like a powerful drug lessening her discomfort. Her pussy cries hotly at being so left out of the action; at feeling so empty compared to her mouth, which technically wasn't even made for his penis the way her cunt was. Her nose smothered in his scrotum, Mira breathes in the scent of his skin like an elixir. She swallows his erection's tender sword, and the point metaphorically pierces her heart – the excruciating experience is thrilling because she truly loves him.

When his penis slides out of her mouth she gasps to fill her lungs with air, surprised and rather awed by her ability to swallow him whole without choking. He slips out of her slowly allowing her time to savor the full length of his cock caressing parts of her no man has ever reached before. She sees him stand up, but before she can begin to feel abandoned, he adjusts the lever beneath the cushion and raises her head level with her body again. Her cheeks are flushed, and her awareness of everything feels relaxed and open in an arousing way. It seems right that her hands and arms are raised as if in supplication or worship or both, because she just worshiped him and now a part of her is silently pleading with him to reward her efforts. Her pussy is open and aching for him. Her cunt's juicy feast is offered up for his cock to begin carving her up and serving them both the pleasure she can't get enough of. On the other hand, she suspects it is too soon in the test for him to reward her by making a hot little red star of her clitoris. He has moved out of her line of sight, and she is just beginning to seriously miss him when he appears again, but only for an instant.

'Oh, no,' she moans as a blindfold falls over her eyes.

'Oh, yes.'

As always the caress of his deep, quiet voice assuages her ruffled emotions. If he says 'oh, yes,' then 'oh, yes' it is. Another small eternity seems to pass as she lies there in her supplicating pose, and the position turns her on so much she feels as if she is begging all the angels above to follow Lucifer down and fuck her one by one... then suddenly she suffers the sweet, deep relief of his cock sliding into her pussy. She moans in gratitude, and then again in frustration desperately wishing she could see him. She could never have foreseen what an exciting new dimension would be added to the pleasure of his penetrations by the straps and chains holding her legs wide open. She cannot defend herself from his thrusts; she cannot control the angle or depth of his penetrations; her hole is forced to absolutely accept his relentless strokes, and the sensation is devastating… her cries rise eloquently around them, letting him know how much she loves being violently stabbed by his erection, and especially how much she loves the excruciating fact that she cannot defend herself from it. Once again relief and disappointment define the nature of her heartbeats as he pulls out of her almost immediately, letting her know there is much more to come and that her first major test as a sex slave has only just begun.

* * *

Master and I spent the night with a submissive slave in training I met online. As usual her boyfriend (master?) was busy (a man who spends three hours working out at the gym every single night instead of spending time with his girlfriend and wanna be slave needs to get his priorities worked out) but she was anxious to meet us (and I was anxious to offer another female body to the altar of our bed) so Master and I met her for dinner at a nice restaurant. We bought her drinks at the bar while we waited for our table, and while her conversation remained stimulating as ever, I found my gaze wandering to another girl dressed in tight black leather pants and a red halter. She was the type I liked to feed Master and me, whereas Julie was rather short and dumpy. Although her face was pretty enough, as was her soft auburn hair, her conservative attire – a gray cardigan and a flower-print skirt long enough to have been worn at the turn of the century – were not a turn on. Master commanded us to go the bathroom and take a picture of each other, and Julie was more than willing to expose her big breasts so I could lick her nipple, and then of her own accord she lifted her skirt so I could photograph her sex before I raised my boot onto the handicap bar and exposed my pussy to the flash.

I ordered grilled Swordfish with corn and tomato salsa and it tasted much better than the conversation, which was all about Julie and her recalcitrant boyfriend. Master and I gave her all the advice we could, and when it was getting time to leave, I apologized for forgetting to bring the books I had promised her.

'You can come home with us so Missa can give you her books,' my Master suggested, 'and then you can watch her suck my cock.'

I didn't think she was going to accept the invitation – but I was wrong. She followed us home in her car, tailing behind us so closely I was afraid she was going to hit us. Once in the living room, Master commanded me to take off my shirt and kneel before him and suck his cock. Julie was sitting on the couch beside him, and when I glanced up at her face in the midst of going down on his towering erection, I had to choke back a laugh. I am not exaggerating when I say that her tongue was lolling hungrily out of her mouth. She was panting with lust in a way that was almost comical in its cartoon-like intensity, making it obvious her boyfriend spent way too much time pumping iron and not enough time pumping her. She was so desperate for my Master's cock she barely gave him time to ask, 'Would you like to help Missa suck me?' before she literally pounced on his hard-on like a starving animal. I sat back on my heels and watched her slurping and swallowing, my hand over my mouth to stifle my laughter as Master and I grinned into each other's eyes.

Eventually, he commanded Julie to sit on the couch while I knelt before her and briefly licked her clit as he fucked me from behind. Then she and I reversed positions and I helped Master slip on a condom and slide his cock inside her pussy. She made an effort to go down on me while he banged her, but she was so overwhelmed she couldn't keep her head up as she cried out helplessly beneath his onslaught. I caressed her breasts (by far her best feature) asking her if he was fucking her too hard, and she shook her head violently, beyond words. Master and I smiled at each other the whole time he was banging her, relishing her complete helplessness in our hands, and then he pulled out of her and led us both into his bathroom. I couldn't believe it when he commanded our totally pliant little guest to kneel in the tub, and I was even more astonished when she promptly obeyed him. I will never forget her utterly lost, starved look as I held my Master's cock in my hand so he could pee all over her naked body.

'Consider this your baptism,' I told her, feeling gloriously at one with him and with his power pressed up against him as he allowed me to control where the scepter of his erection rained his clean, warm urine all over another girl's naked flesh. She had gone from not being allowed to be alone with us to letting another man piss all over her breasts and belly and legs.

Afterwards, we let her rinse herself off, and then back out in the bedroom, Master and I both caressed her where she lay between us. Then he commanded me to assume the sleen position, and instructed Julie to lick my ass and ready it for his cock. She didn't comply with this request, her eyes at last showing signs of concerned life, so he told her to just watch closely while he reamed me. I pulled her up beneath me to lick her pussy as he fucked my tight sphincter, moaning with effort and pleasure as I raised myself up to lick and fondle her breasts while he came explosively in my rectum.

Pleasantly spent, the three of us lay on the bed talking. 'Missa has such beautiful hair,' she told my Master, 'and such lips... so Egyptian.'

I gave her a copy of some of my books, we escorted her down to her car, and then Master and I contentedly walked Merlin together.

The following morning, Master said to me as we were lying in bed, 'I have such a good life.'

'Mm,' I replied. 'I love the way you completely devastate all the girls you fuck.'

CHAPTER TEN

Rituals of Surrender

realize the objective 'they' known as society might categorize me as a bit of a control freak. The living space I share with my Master is always clean and neat; both my hard-copy and electronic files are organized in folders; I have a notebook in the kitchen filled with all my favorite recipes which I either cut out of books or type myself on the computer as I create them, then I print them and tape them into a ruled notebook divided into different sections – Sandwiches, Seafood, Chicken, Pasta, etc.; I adore the organized fullness of my linen closet; all my clothes are arranged by season, color, and type, with all my fetish attire, stockings, garters and sexy panties occupying their own chest of drawers; my kitchen invariably looks good enough to be the set of a cooking show; I write everything I need to do on my desk calendar; all my bills are paid long before the due date and I never fail to have stamps on hand for those I can't dispose of online; as a member of *Netflix* Master and I always have DVD's available to entertain us at night; our wine racks are usually overflowing, and there are always two vintages of chardonnay along with a bottle of champagne chilling in the refrigerator.

Obviously, I like to be prepared for things, because in my opinion that's the best way to enjoy them to the fullest. Unlike the infamous Blanche, I have no desire to rely on the kindness of strangers, feeling I can do a better job of most everything myself; I don't trust most people to be as intensely discriminating as I am. I believe that, as a general rule, people are good, but I am more skeptical about them as individuals I can relate to for a prolonged period of time.

Master is the exception to every rule in my personal universe. When we're together, the only control I have and desire is my ability to express how much I love him. Early on in our relationship, Master and I had a conversation. I don't recall it verbatim, but it went something like this:

'Do you like to cook, Missa?' he asked.

'Yes, I suppose I do. I can't say that I love it, but I do insist on enjoying my meals every night, and since I can't afford to eat out all the time, I cook. Also, I could never maintain my weight or my health if I ate out all the time. This way I know exactly what I'm putting into my body.'

'You're in full control.'

'Yes.'

'I'll allow you that control in the kitchen, and in your writing, and in your domestic chores,' he stated as casually as if we were merely discussing the weather, 'but when it comes to us, you will surrender that control completely and absolutely without question.'

I took a deep breath as if to protest, and then realized with a shocking thrill that the only words lined up in my head and lodged in my throat ready to emerge were, 'Yes, Master.'

* * *

It rarely happens now, but many times when Master commanded me to take my clothes off I really didn't want to because I was feeling fat or bloated, either from eating or because it was that time of the month. 'If I see you as beautiful, then you are beautiful, Missa,' he told me sternly on countless occasions, and the truth of this statement has at last become a part of me. It's amazing how knotted up our thoughts and emotions can be, so that very often we have no idea why we react the way we do to things. So much of my relationship with Master has been about patiently untangling the threads of my psyche. For example, one evening when he knelt between my legs where I sat on the love seat, preparing to go down on me, I was filled with irrational resentment, and in a surly tone informed him that I was tired, using this as en excuse for my frigid reaction because I just didn't feel like making the effort to feel beautiful and sexy and have an orgasm; therefore, I felt guilty that I would be wasting his time if I allowed him to procede. I went dead inside in that terrible way I once suffered, and I used being physically tired as an excuse. He had already told me more than once that he loves going down on me, and that I should never feel pressured to come, but thanks to a former emotionally abusive relationship I was being stupid and thinking he was just making a grand gesture to please me, not really getting anything out of it himself. And then what happened? As soon as I realized what was going on inside me, as soon as I stopped seeing my body as imperfect and let myself experience it through his loving eyes, I relaxed, effortlessly surrendered to the sensual experience, and had a great orgasm. I learned that I truly can be 'sensual on command' if I really want to be and don't let my brain short-circuit my soul.

* * *

I'll never forget the night Master helped me discover the words I need to think or say whenever I am possessed by a blinding emotional pain – Love Goddess. I have mentioned the emotionally abusive relationship I suffered for such a long time, before I finally freed myself of it less then two years before Master entered my life… there are times when part of me (the younger, emotional self) forgets I am with

Master; I forget that when he commands me to do something and to obey him he is not seeking to humiliate me and turn me into a door-mat, he is trying to make me the beautiful slave I want to be, the beautiful Love Goddess he can enjoy worshipping without my wounded self-esteem crippling our devotion to each other as priest and priestess – Master and slave. That night was a revelation. 'Violet' will remain my safe word for physical pain, but 'Love Goddess' is what I will say silently in my head whenever I start to forget who I'm with, who I am now, and who I'm continuing to become like a flower blooms thanks to the depth of our love, which is much more real than the lack of love and respect I lived with for so long.

The night I first used my safe word 'violet' Master and I were alone in our bedroom. I don't recall the details, I just know that I had been suffering a particularly bad case of negativity stemming from God only knows what experiences I had suffered with other men in the past, and Master attempted a novel approach of exor-cizing my demons. After disciplining me with the paddle, he yanked me to my feet, forced me roughly down onto my hands and knees, and rammed his hard-on through my sphincter without warning. It hurt like hell, but my real pain stemmed from what I believed to be his anger with me. 'Violet!' I cried. 'Violet!'

He pulled his erection out of my ass immediately, cradling me tenderly in his arms.

'Why are you so mad at me?' I sobbed.

'I'm not mad at you, Missa…'

'Yes, you are! You were trying to hurt me!'

'No, I wasn't. Listen to me, I'm not mad at you and I wasn't try-ing to hurt you… I was trying to take you over the edge… you've been complaining that I'm too gentle with you, that you need more discipline… I thought I could push you over an edge where you would be able to turn the pain into pleasure. I'm sorry I hurt you. I've never been mad at you, and I can see how whatever I did would hurt you if you thought I was mad at you. I may have been annoyed and impatient with you at times, but I've never been mad.'

'But you weren't looking at me… I need you to look at me… I realize all my fears center around you not looking at me, Master, when you're disciplining me, when we're swinging, I always need you to look at me…'

'Very good, Missa, you have no idea what you just spared yourself. You always get it exactly right, and keep us on course.'

'Your eyes have all the power I always dreamed of, Master.'

After the emotional storm had been cleared up by my Magic word, he put on a condom because his dick had just been in my ass, and while he fucked me, I found it perversely exciting to feel like a girl he was swinging with; it turned me on to know how they had all felt and would feel, and to know there wasn't anything he hadn't done to them he hadn't also done to me now.

Now, whenever Master senses me suffering a lack of faith in our relationship, whenever he senses me questioning our love and my commitment to being his slave, he says, 'Kneel and reflect' and I must immediately stop whatever I am doing and sink to my knees with my head lowered and my hands lying face-up on my knees as I reflect on my actions and attitude, until I find my peaceful, contented center as Missa again. This simple ritual works wonders, and I am very grateful to my Master for his penetrating understanding of my emotional being which inspired him to create it.

Yet even after nearly three years together, I was still discovering tiny but potentially fatal cracks in my psyche. After the Martini Saturday before he left for a short business trip, I realized what was killing me – I was still suffering from a lack of faith in our love in that I didn't trust him one hundred percent. I trusted him ninety-nine percent, but that one percent was like a vacuum leak into space in which I was still faced with the threat of emptiness and loneliness forever and ever without love, and that's why I was afraid. And he was right when he said that one missing percent was eating away at the amazing love and trust that exists between us just like a vacuum threatening to suck everything out into it. Right before he goes away on a trip, I make an effort to detach myself from him to avoid the pain of missing him, and it was then that one percent of mistrust became bigger and bigger as I looked for any excuse to detach myself from him. The intense clarity of Vodka made that profound gap in my faith glaringly obvious, which is good, because it enabled me to see that I didn't really completely trust him like I thought I did, and that's why I was still afraid of certain things; afraid that in some way he would hurt me eventually, and I would be alone again lost in an intolerably empty space, this time forever, because I can never love another man the way I love my Master. He is the man I was made for.

One night shortly before that, Master left me tied up on my bed (he had good reason to) and went to walk Merlin, at which point thousands of years of genetic programming compelled me to break free of my bonds and to be proud of my ability to do so. Part of me felt compelled to resist my desire to put my life in his hands, the ultimate act of love and a defiant transcendence of society's evils. The following day he chained me to the bed and left me there on the floor for a long time, and this time I was at peace leaning against the bed and gazing at the pillow on the love seat, my mind remarkably and blessedly free of thoughts. Merlin visited me once, excited to see me sitting on his level, then left (probably to go sleep near Master) and I was alone again. When Master finally returned, he smiled at me approvingly and unlocked the chain as he said, 'Have you realized now that nothing is more important than waiting for me, Missa?'

'Yes, Master,' I replied, and it was true.

There can be no limit to how much I trust my Master. My trust in him is absolute and includes the largest and smallest of my fears and anxieties. How many women can say that about their husbands?

* * *

There were a few months there when Master was disciplining me regularly – almost every night.

'What do you say, Missa?' he asked, the dreaded paddle he forged for this task hovering over my bare ass.

'May I have another, please, Master?'

'Yes, you may.'

I asked for three more blows, each one harder than the last, and it was excruciating and yet wonderful.

'Let your spirit flow with me, Missa. I love it when you confess things to me, but you're better at denying than admitting.' On this particular night, I had reacted in a defensive, surly way to a porno film of two girls having sex, denying the fact that it was turning me on. The truth is my pussy was getting all warm and wet watching two girls play with each other's sex, but I was afraid to admit it because I didn't want my arousal at that moment to imply that I was eventually going to break down and become a lesbian. It's embarrassing how many times I've been afraid to light a match because I was afraid of burning down the whole house.

Master fucked me twice in a row after letting me choose my instrument of punishment – the short riding crop – and I came twice. Afterwards he said, 'I'm all fucked out' and we were.

Yet it wasn't until we were vacationing in Toronto that he at last answered the question I had asked him out loud several times, and which I had been silently asking myself ever since he collared me. One afternoon in our hotel room, when I was giving him an attitude, he said, 'Missa, you're the slave and I'm the Master.'

'Yes,' I replied, staring intently up into his eyes, 'but what does that mean, exactly?'

'It means our life isn't going to be ruled by your emotions.'

My heart seemed to expand with relief that at long last he had given me the answer I was so desperately seeking. 'Master, that was finally the right answer,' I said, tears of relief and gratitude in my eyes. He had finally broken the code; he had at last solved the riddle over the temple door and gained us full admittance. 'Thank you, Master.'

* * *

We will be moving again soon, leaving Northern Virginia and heading deep south to Louisiana where we hope to buy a house with lots of land for privacy where I can add growing my own vegetables and herbs, grilling, swimming, kayaking, relaxing in a hot tub and entertaining both in our dining room and in our dream 'dungeon' to the already extensive list of all the pleasures we enjoy together.

I like to imagine that the following excerpt from *The Fabric of Love* (the Lords willing) could be a fictional reflection of the pages of my diary a year or two from now:

A few hours later Stormy and Sekhmet have explored Phillip's house from top to bottom several times, not including the cellar, from which they are forever banned. The evening is unnaturally cool for early August in Virginia, and it is all the excuse Phillip and Mira need to strip naked and step into the hot tub where they sit across from each other. A filet mignon roast and too large Idaho potatoes are cooking in the oven, and the cold white wine flowing onto her tongue is a delicious contrast to the embracing heat of the water. The sun has sunk below the horizon but it isn't dark yet, and the sight of her Master's handsome face framed by the beauty of his yard at twilight is all she can possibly ask of life as she takes another inspiring sip of chardonnay. Every relaxing moment she spends with him is promisingly pregnant with all the sensual feasts they will share in every sense.

'I'm so glad you're here,' he tells her quietly. 'You make me very happy, Mira.'

The deep, penetrating look in his eyes is the very heart of the universe for her; everything lives in and for him. His awareness, his soul is the reason she was born and took form and developed a visual cortex so her being could gaze into his like this. Together they are the reason for everything mysteriously delivered in an envelope of flesh, and the closer they become, the more they open up to each other, the more every day and every night feels like a love letter written in blood from the heart of the cosmos. 'Do you believe in the soul, Phillip?'

'You know I do, Mira.'

'I just can't imagine dying and never seeing you again...'

'Then don't imagine it.'

She smiles, sadness and happiness battling in her pulse. 'Yes, Master.'

'I've had certain... experiences that can only be explained by the possibility that I've lived before,' he confesses.

'Really? Such as?'

'I'll tell you about them some other time, not tonight. Suffice it to say that I definitely believe there's such a thing as a soul that survives the death of the body.'

As if in response to his assertion of immortality two black streaks soar erratically over their heads. 'Oh, look, bats!' she exclaims happily. It is much darker now; the leaves of the trees are almost indistinguishable from the sky, and soon only the porch's halo of light will reveal individual flowers and bushes. Mira took it upon herself to light all the gas lamps so the night would not swallow them up as they sat in the hot tub. A powerful jet of water is massaging her lower back, and she lifts her right foot in search of some aquatic reflexology, all the time holding her glass of chardonnay above the frothing water. 'Mm…' The hard bubbles beating against the sole of her foot somehow help relax her entire body. 'I understand now why Chinese concubines were treated to foot rubs with little circular mallets,' she muses out loud, 'but only on the night their lord had chosen to spend with them as a reward for being in his favor.'

'Tell me more.' He sounds intrigued.

'I don't know much more really, I've never particularly cared for the Chinese culture; I much prefer the Japanese and the Hindus.'

'Oh, yes, Tantric sex… that's something else we should explore in the future, not anytime soon, though; we're not ready for that yet.'

'It's wonderful having things to look forward to, isn't it?' She sets her glass down on the tub's wooden platform in favor of sinking even lower into the hot foam and subjecting her other foot to a jet's teasingly inconsistent massage. 'I could never be just another concubine,' she continues thinking out loud, something she can do with her Master she was never really able to do with anyone else. 'I could never share your love and attention with other women, but then love has had very little to do with marriage throughout most of history.' She glances at him uncertainly, regretting her use of the word 'marriage' afraid he might take it personally. They have known each other less than three months; it is definitely too soon to even discuss such a possibility.

'I understand you couldn't share my love with other women,' he says, and pauses to drain his glass, 'but what about occasionally sharing my body?'

'That's different,' she replies, too busy riding a wave of relief that he didn't even blink at her Freudian slip to think about it. 'In ancient Egypt there was only one wife and all the other women in the household were either servants or concubines... not that I would like that either; I wouldn't want other women around all the time.'

'That's perfectly understandable, and there never will be, but I'm very proud of you for grasping the difference between loving someone and fucking them.'

'When we first met, I was very jealous of the women you dominate, but I'm not anymore, not like I used to be, anyway. I know they don't mean anything to you, not like I do.' She sits up and reaches for her wine again. 'But are you saying that sex and love have nothing to do with each other?' The darkness around them suddenly feels threatening rather than promising.

'Not at all, when you have sex with the person you love,

you're making love, not just fucking.'

'Then why was the Chief Wife in ancient Egypt not allowed the same sexual freedom as her husband?' she demands, centuries of oppression fueling her retort.

'Because he had to make sure those were his babies she was breeding, not some other man's. It had everything to do with preserving the bloodline and the political power that went with it. In the ancient Egypt of the future, things will be different.'

She laughs. 'I like that, an ancient Egypt of the future… it would be a wonderful place to live.'

'And we've already begun laying the foundations for such a sensually enlightened society, my beautiful slave.'

'But it would also have to be an intensely spiritual society,' she points out, shying away from the glorification of superficial hedonism. 'And I'm not talking institutionalized religion here.'

'Mira,' he sets his empty glass down on the tub's wooden lip, 'to be enlightened implies a certain depth of mind and spirit. When I say "sensually enlightened" I'm not talking about the Playboy castle, I'm talking about integrating all aspects of our being, which is a sacred art and the only true pleasure to be had in life as we know it.'

She carefully discards her own glass again, and wades across the waves into his arms. 'You are the smartest, wisest man I have ever met, Master.' She plants her lips against his. They taste better to her everyday as a result of all the fascinating thoughts and concepts he expresses with them, and tonight they're slick from being kissed by hot foam as well as tartly sweet from the chardonnay. She loses herself in his mouth for timeless moments, playing contentedly with his tongue, and then wrestling with it more urgently as she feels his penis hardening between her thighs.

She pulls back. 'Do you love me, Master?'

'You know I do, Mira.' Beneath the water his hands wrap her legs fully around his hips. 'I love you more than anything,' he adds intently, positioning the swollen head of his cock at the entrance to her flesh. 'You're the most important thing in the world to me, never forget it.'

'But what about when I'm old and ugly?' she asks breathlessly as his hard-on slips into her cunt and fills her up as only he can.

'You'll never be ugly!' he says through his teeth, jamming his cock even deeper into her pussy and leaving no room inside her for doubts.

'But I'll be old,' she insists, 'and how can I be a beautiful sex slave when I'm old?' She knows she is being perversely needy and begging for his reassurance, but she doesn't care; she needs him more than anything and she is afraid her growing happiness will be cruelly cut down one day for some reason or other.

'We'll both be old,' he points out, 'and you'll be even more beautiful in my eyes than ever, and I'll still be your Master and the love of your life, won't I.' His fingers gripping her ass are silent, indelible statements she has no desire to argue with as he holds her down around his erection and thrusts urgently up beneath her. 'For a deep and intelligent woman, you can be very silly sometimes, Mira. Wires grow old and eventually burn out, but the energy that traveled through them is unaffected. How can you possibly think that our love will dim with time?'

'I didn't say that,' she moans as his hands now clutch her

hips and force her pussy up and down his rigid length.

'Yes, you did say that.'

'Oh, God, no, I didn't!' she cries, holding on to his slick shoulders. She resents the rushing heat of the water that does not allow her to fully feel him, and the chemically-treated foam is competing with her vagina's natural juices and winning. Their genitals are completely underwater yet his greedy shaft has to ram past her dry opening into the moist interior.

'Are you arguing with your Master?' he demands.

'No, Master, I'm sorry…'

'What's wrong?' He studies her face. 'Don't you like having my cock inside you?'

'I love your cock inside me, Master, but… it doesn't feel as good in here.'

He slides her tight hole off his dick. 'Come on.' He takes her hand, and side-by-side they climb the steps out of the hot tub.

The porch is a dry golden haven of gas lamps and candle light and a large wicker couch covered with water-proof cushions. He seats himself, and she knows he wants her to keep riding him, but she isn't yet wet enough on the inside.

'May I touch myself, Master?' she asks, standing before him.

'Yes, you may,' he replies.

She shivers. The night feels even colder than it really is to her flushed skin, but the tremor that courses down her spine has much more to do with the look in his eyes and with the sight of his hands cradling his generous balls and stroking his ideal erection as he looks at her. She doesn't feel at all shy tonight. With her hair half dry and half wet, black tendrils clinging snake-like to her taut breasts, light-jeweled drops of water caressing her body all the slow way down her belly and legs, the candle light gilding her smooth skin to a flawless, ageless perfection, she feels timelessly beautiful as she crushes her clit beneath her fingertips and firmly coaxes her pussy into juicing. Her clit is another wick coming to warm life on the porch and igniting that sweet, greedy tension in her pelvis which can so easily lead to the devastating conflagration of a climax. In a matter of seconds, she is ready for him. She straddles him, her knees sinking into the cushions on either side of him, and takes possession of his erection to guide it slowly inside her. She wants to savor the experience of his hard-on's demanding dimensions opening her up, and she also wants him to watch his cock parting the folds of her labia and slowly disappearing into her warm, embracing slot. Only when his penis is packed inside her to the hilt does she brace herself on his shoulders − as straight and broad as any pharaoh's − and begin massaging his cock with her pussy muscles as she rides him, working her cunt swiftly up and down around him.

'Keep touching yourself,' he commands.

She moans, only interested in pleasing him at the moment.

'I told you to touch yourself, Mira.'

She obeys of course, and forgets her reluctance, wondering why she ever felt it in the first place as her fingertips work her clitoris like the magic button of her sensual wiring. Her hips selfishly orbit the climax building inside her, his rampant penis the motionless center of the beautiful storm in her nerve-endings.

'That's it, make yourself come,' he urges quietly, caressing her breasts and gently pinching her nipples.

Up until that moment she was concentrating on the pulsing

wick of a candle burning in a bronze lamp hanging from the ceiling, but now she looks down into his eyes, and ecstasy mysteriously unravels her from the inside out as she sees all the flames reflected back at her in his penetratingly dark irises.

'Mm,' he says after she finally descends from the blindingly beautiful realm of her orgasm. 'Get up.'

She is literally weak in the knees, the warm glow in her sex relaxing all her other muscles so that it takes her longer than it normally would to lift herself off him, stand up, and then position herself on her hands and knees on the cushions. He kneels behind her, and she tosses her head as he penetrates her, flinging her hair across her back so he can grab its mane as he swiftly rides her to his own pounding climax.

'Mreow!' Sekhmet materializes from the shadows. She assumes the statuesque pose of her namesake and stares up at the two naked human bodies pretending to be cats with eyes the same burning yellow of the flames illuminating her like a sacred icon.

Mira returns her stare, not sure if her feline's eyes are blazing with jealousy or cold with contempt or if her regard is, somehow, fiercely approving. She sits down beside her Master on the couch and rests her head on his chest, cuddling up against him for warmth as they both gaze back at the cat.

'Well, Sekhmet,' he says, 'do you and your brother approve of your soon-to-be new territory?'

She turns her head.

Stormy slinks out from the cover of another shadow and rubs his purring body up against his sister's.

She hisses and swats him with her paw, but her claws are sheathed, betraying her secret fondness for him.

He removes himself to a safer distance and begins licking his penis, his hind leg thrust comically straight up into the air.

'They love it,' Mira translates. 'I'm getting cold. Can we go inside, Master?'

'Yes, we may.'

'I'll get the wine glasses.'

'No, just leave them. I have plenty more, and there's still some wine left in yours that will serve as an offering.'

'As an offering to what?' she asks, intrigued.

He shrugs as they get up. 'Whatever's out there... there are unseen forces all around us, Mira, best to keep them on our side.'

'Yes!' she agrees, and walks gratefully into the warmer embrace of the house as he opens the screen door for her. 'Dinner should be ready soon. May I put something on to serve, Master?'

'Yes, I suppose you may. It's getting chilly and I'd like to eat outside, if that's all right with you. We'll be cooped up inside long enough during the winter.'

'I love eating outside.'

'Mm... and I love eating you.' He pulls her into his arms and kisses her. 'But I suppose that will have to wait until later.' He lets go of her just as abruptly. 'I don't want you burning our dinner.'

She follows him upstairs. The climb to his tower bedroom never fails to leave her a bit winded, and she wonders if she'll ever get used to it. He heads for the shower to rinse off, but she contents herself with the soft hug of a large Egyptian cotton towel before slipping into a pair of black cotton house pants, and a violet shirt with long sleeves that end in tulip-like ruffles that cover her upper hands Medieval-style. And because he has given her permission to wear clothing, it means she does not have to wear high-heels while moving about in the kitchen and carrying a heavy tray out onto the porch. Soft black 'ballet' slippers are just what her feet need to hurry back down the tower stairs, at the bottom of which Stormy and Sekhmet both greet her vociferously.

'Yes, yes, I know, it's past your dinner time,' she apologizes happily. 'But don't worry, I brought your bowls and your favorite canned tuna.' Her devoted (hungry) entourage follows her into the kitchen, which still takes her breath away with its utterly efficient beauty. She knows where everything is already, and has not quite gotten over marveling at a straight man with such excellent taste in plates and stemware. The stainless steel side-by-side refrigerator was going sadly to waste before she came along, but now its clean white plastic bowels are at least modestly filled with food. Once she and her Master live together, and she is not dividing groceries between their two homes, this dream refrigerator will be bursting with cheeses and condiments and fruits and vegetables and meats and everything else needed for a sensually enlightened existence, which naturally includes regular orgasms of the taste buds by way of excellent nutrition.

She takes the roast out of the oven, and thrusts the metal tip of an electronic meat thermometer into the thickest part of the filet, watching anxiously as the temperature on the display escalates. She sincerely hopes she did not overdo it, but sometimes it's hard balancing gourmet cooking with great sex, a demanding task she is more than happy to live with.

'Meow! Meow! Meow!' Sekhmet is letting her know #she# is always supposed to come first.

'I'm coming!' The temperature of the roast is perfect. She tents it loosely beneath tinfoil so it will finish cooking while releasing more of its delicious internal juices. 'Okay.' She quickly opens two cans of tuna, a task made much easier by an electric can opener, and quickly dishes the feast out into two separate bowls. 'See, it's just like we're at home,' she says, and as she straightens up from feeding her cats, Mira realizes it's true, they are at home, in her Master's castle, and as long as they live she'll never feel that cold, paralyzing loneliness in her soul again. 'You have no idea how lucky we are, babies,' she says, but her words fall on ears deafened by the greedy smacking of the jaws beneath them.

She has just finished loading the large wicker tray with plates, napkins, glasses, forks and steak knives when her Master enters the kitchen, as usual looking intensely sexy even though he's very casually dressed in black slippers, black sweat pants and a black sweatshirt. He steps up behind her and slips his arms around her waist as she lifts the foil off the filet mignon.

'Mm!' He buries his face in her damp hair. 'That looks fabulous.'

'Thank you, Master, but timing is critical here; I really need to serve this right away.'

'Which means I'd better hurry down to the cellar for a bottle of wine.'

'Yes, and please hurry, Master. I'll meet you out on the porch.'

'Want to just have one of mom and dad's bottles tonight?'

'Sure, that would be great. I love your parents' wine.'

'And they'll love you, my slave. I've already told them I'm getting married.'

She nearly drops the tray.

'Not any time soon, mind you, I want to get my PhD first, and continue your training before we take that conventional step, but it will happen Mira, you know that, and when the time comes, I'll ask you properly.'

They both stand perfectly still gazing at each other while she holds the tray up between them like an offering, and the longer they just stand there lost in each other's eyes, the more the silver and the crystal and the fine fabric placemats and napkins begin to feel like symbols of everything they can possibly desire together. There are only two words she needs to speak, only two words she needs to utter to express everything she has always believed deep in her soul and everything she is daring to feel, only two words which say it all and which no one can prove untrue in the universe that is all theirs, 'Yes, Master.'

CONCLUSION
Not Written in Stone

An old soul experiences everything as fresh in each life because it's always contained in a body designed to do just that by way of developing senses and perceptions. In a similar way two souls who have met and been in love before experience each other as if for the first time in a different body of circumstances.

The fluid atmosphere of life consists of degrees of pleasure encompassing the whole of a human being's faculties, not just the physical senses. Making my bed with cotton jersey sheets instead of flannel sheets for the warmer weather in spring is just one of the many sensual pleasures I enjoy that all flow into each other like pearls on a necklace. To imagine that a Master and slave relationship entails mostly bondage, discipline and sex is to have a one-dimensional view of reality. For the most part, Master and I live a private, intimate life together just like so-called normal people, the difference is we are open to sharing experiences most married and monogamous couples are either not interested in or deny themselves for some reason or other.

One night as we were relaxing in front of the television, I asked, 'Do you like having three orifices always available to you at a second's notice, Master?'

'Like it?' he replied. 'It's part of my life. I love it.'

The problem with writing a memoir is that you grow and yet your thoughts and feelings remain carved in print stone. When I go back and read certain passages from *The Story of M – A Memoir* I cringe a little. I have developed a great deal as a person and as a slave since I penned those sentences and I no longer feel exactly the same way about everything I wrote. I can only hope my readers will realize that M was a description of my first year of training with my Master and that things just keep getting better if you continue growing. I will say, however, that all fantasies need to be tempered by reality. Master and I have done this, and are in much better control of our fantasies as a result of having dared to live them together. In the process, we have defined what works and doesn't work for us and what we desire to continue experiencing together in the future.

When I first became my Master's slave I was like a rookie cop who folded at the first sign of blood – the death of all I had believed about monogamy and true love. I felt as if I was playing with snakes like the topless statuettes of a Minoan goddess who kept getting bitten by doubts and fears. Our more quiet life in Virginia helped balance our excessively hedonistic life in Miami. Experience and learn… I look back with pride at all that Master and I have done together and on what it has taught us about each other as individuals and as a couple striving to become one.

Shortly after our second anniversary, Master forged a silver collar for me which locks with a tiny silver heart to which only he has the key. I graduated from my black leather training collar to this, my official collar, which he made for me with his own hands.

'My flesh is bound to yours,' he said, 'you can't ever die.'

In the end terms like boyfriend and girlfriend, husband and wife, Master and slave, are just words, what matters is the love; how much you love each other and strive to make each other happy. What matters is where you go and what you do, not the conceptual vehicle you do it in. Master and slave happens to be our preferred method of life travel, and the main purpose of this book is to try and show people that it's as valid a way of getting around the infinitely intriguing realm of love as any more traditional forms of transportation. It is no more ridiculous to be an octogenarian Master and slave couple than it is to be an octogenarian husband and wife, partner and significant other, whatever. Love does not age, and while certain rituals may fall by the wayside like leaves shed in autumn, whatever the framework of the relationship two people in love choose for each other, even when all the leaves of their lives' moments have fallen away, the naked lines of their relationship remain.

Quoted Sources:

1 *True Magick – A Beginner's Guide*, ©1990 by Amber K., Llewellyn Publications

2 Discovery Issue Volume 25, No. 5, *Antonio Damasio's Theory of Thinking Faster and Faster*, by Steven Johnson

3 Discovery Issue Volume 25, No. 5, *Here Comes The Sun*, by Dana Mackenzie

4 *The Occult*, © Colin Wilson 2003, Watkins Publishing, originally published by Grafton Books, 1979

Maria Isabel Pita is the author of three erotic BDSM novels – *Thorsday Night, Eternal Bondage, To Her Master Born* (re-printed as an exclusive hard-cover edition by the Doubleday Venus Book Club) and four erotic romances – *Dreams of Anubis, Pleasures Unknown, Recipe For Romance* and *The Fabric of Love*. She is also the author of the non-fiction book, *The Story of M – A Memoir*, the vividly detailed account of her first year of training as a slave to her Master and soul mate continued in Beauty & Submission. Maria lives with her beloved Master, Stinger, and their dog, Merlin. You can visit her at www.mariaisabelpita.com